Child Development and International Development: Research–Policy Interfaces

Daniel A. Wagner, *Editor*

NEW DIRECTIONS FOR CHILD DEVELOPMENT
WILLIAM DAMON, *Editor-in-Chief*

Number 20, June 1983

Paperback sourcebooks in
The Jossey-Bass Social and Behavioral Sciences Series

Jossey-Bass Inc., Publishers
San Francisco • Washington • London

Daniel A. Wagner (Ed.).
Child Development and International Development: Research-Policy Interfaces.
New Directions for Child Development, no. 20.
San Francisco: Jossey-Bass, 1983.

New Directions for Child Development Series
William Damon, *Editor-in-Chief*

Copyright © 1983 by Jossey-Bass Inc., Publishers
and
Jossey-Bass Limited

Copyright under International, Pan American, and Universal
Copyright Conventions. All rights reserved. No part of
this issue may be reproduced in any form—except for brief
quotation (not to exceed 500 words) in a review or professional
work—without permission in writing from the publishers.

New Directions for Child Development (publication number
USPS 494-090) is published quarterly by Jossey-Bass Inc., Publishers.
Second-class postage rates are paid at San Francisco, California,
and at additional mailing offices.

Correspondence:
Subscriptions, single-issue orders, change of address notices,
undelivered copies, and other correspondence should be sent to
New Directions Subscriptions, Jossey-Bass Inc., Publishers,
433 California Street, San Francisco, California 94104.

Editorial correspondence should be sent to the Editor-in-Chief,
William Damon, Department of Psychology, Clark University,
Worcester, Massachusetts 01610.

Library of Congress Catalogue Card Number LC 82-82181
International Standard Serial Number ISSN 0195-2269
International Standard Book Number ISBN 87589-932-3

Cover art by Willi Baum
Manufactured in the United States of America

Ordering Information

The paperback sourcebooks listed below are published quarterly and can be ordered either by subscription or single-copy.

Subscriptions cost $35.00 per year for institutions, agencies, and libraries. Individuals can subscribe at the special rate of $21.00 per year *if payment is by personal check*. (Note that the full rate of $35.00 applies if payment is by institutional check, even if the subscription is designated for an individual.) Standing orders are accepted. Subscriptions normally begin with the first of the four sourcebooks in the current publication year of the series. When ordering, please indicate if you prefer your subscription to begin with the first issue of the *coming* year.

Single copies are available at $7.95 when payment accompanies order, and *all single-copy orders under $25.00 must include payment*. (California, New Jersey, New York, and Washington, D.C., residents please include appropriate sales tax.) For billed orders, cost per copy is $7.95 plus postage and handling. (Prices subject to change without notice.)

Bulk orders (ten or more copies) of any individual sourcebook are available at the following discounted prices: 10–49 copies, $7.15 each; 50–100 copies, $6.35 each; over 100 copies, *inquire*. Sales tax and postage and handling charges apply as for single copy orders.

To ensure correct and prompt delivery, all orders must give either the *name of an individual* or an *official purchase order number*. Please submit your order as follows:

Subscriptions: specify series and year subscription is to begin.
Single Copies: specify sourcebook code (such as, CD8) and first two words of title.

Mail orders for United States and Possessions, Latin America, Canada, Japan, Australia, and New Zealand to:
Jossey-Bass Inc., Publishers
433 California Street
San Francisco, California 94104

Mail orders for all other parts of the world to:
Jossey-Bass Limited
28 Banner Street
London EC1Y 8QE

New Directions for Child Development Series
William Damon, *Editor-in-Chief*

CD1 *Social Cognition,* William Damon
CD2 *Moral Development,* William Damon
CD3 *Early Symbolization,* Howard Gardner, Dennie Wolf
CD4 *Social Interaction and Communication During Infancy,* Ina C. Uzgiris
CD5 *Intellectual Development Beyond Childhood,* Deanna Kuhn
CD6 *Fact, Fiction, and Fantasy in Childhood,* Ellen Winner, Howard Gardner

CD7 *Clinical-Developmental Psychology,* Robert L. Selman, Regina Yando
CD8 *Anthropological Perspectives on Child Development,* Charles M. Super, Sara Harkness
CD9 *Children's Play,* Kenneth H. Rubin
CD10 *Children's Memory,* Marion Perlmutter
CD11 *Developmental Perspectives on Child Maltreatment,* Ross Rizley, Dante Cicchetti
CD12 *Cognitive Development,* Kurt W. Fisher
CD13 *Viewing Children Through Television,* Hope Kelly, Howard Gardner
CD14 *Childrens' Conceptions of Health, Illness, and Bodily Functions,* Roger Bibace, Mary E. Walsh
CD15 *Children's Conceptions of Spatial Relationships,* Robert Cohen
CD16 *Emotional Development,* Dante Cicchetti, Petra Hesse
CD17 *Developmental Approaches to Giftedness and Creativity,* David Henry Feldman
CD18 *Children's Planning Strategies,* David Forbes, Mark T. Greenberg
CD19 *Children and Divorce,* Lawrence A. Kurdek

Contents

Editor's Notes 1
Daniel A. Wagner
More collaboration is needed between child development researchers and international policy planners.

Chapter 1. Urban Migration in Developing Countries: 5
Consequences for Families and Their Children
Mary Racelis Hollnsteiner, Peter Taçon
Urban migration can provide greater economic opportunity, better health services for families, and better schools for children, but migration can also bring poverty and despair.

Chapter 2. Socioeconomic Determinants of Infant and Child Mortality 27
in Developing Countries
Susan Cochrane, Kalpana Mehra
The determinants of infant and child mortality include many social and economic factors, but deciding which of these factors are the major causes is a difficult question.

Chapter 3. Fertility and Child Development: 45
An Anthropological Approach
Robert A. LeVine
For population education programs to be successful, much more needs to be known about why parents have varying numbers of children. An anthropological approach to the study of fertility considers how cultural beliefs affect childbearing and socialization.

Chapter 4. The Effects of Maternal Employment on Children's Welfare 57
in Rural Guatemala
Patricia A. Engle
Recent evidence suggests that maternal employment may increase the probability of child survival.

Chapter 5. Indigenous Education and Literacy in the Third World 77
Daniel A. Wagner
Traditional Islamic education is one major example of an indigenous institution that may be able to provide literacy and other basic skills to children who do not enter formal public school systems.

Chapter 6. Child Labor and National Development: 87
An Annotated Bibliography
Elizabeth A. Moore

A consensus is needed on how to define the words *child* and *labor*. Views on definitions, values, and perceived needs also vary across societies. This annotated bibliography brings together a selection of research in this area.

Chapter 7. What Policy Relevance Can Mean 107
Francis X. Sutton

This chapter presents a foundation perspective on papers presented at the 1982 AAAS symposium.

Chapter 8. Sources of Additional Information 113
Daniel A. Wagner

Index 117

Editor's Notes

Children, it is sometimes said, are the future—a simple proposition that would be affirmed by diverse peoples in most parts of the world today. To nourish and protect this future necessarily involves the direct participation of many sectors of society. Parents, teachers, and international civil servants are among the many individuals who make the general welfare of children a very high priority. Organizations also provide crucial support services for children through such international public and private agencies as UNESCO, UNICEF, WHO, CARE, and Save the Children. Particularly in the last twenty-five years, these organizations have played a major role in improving the welfare of children by providing health, nutritional, and educational goods and services in many parts of the world.

The geopolitical focus of the present volume is on the developing countries of the Third World. (In this volume, we shall use the terms *Third World* and *developing countries* interchangeably, since these are most commonly used in the literature of development—another problematical concept, for all countries are developing in some fashion.) A dramatic improvement in child survival has been achieved in the Third World. With the construction of clinics, training of paramedical personnel, and development of health education programs, child mortality has dropped by over 50 percent in some parts of the Third World. This noteworthy achievement has been made possible by the collaborative efforts of international organizations and national governments as well as by the personal efforts of midlevel policy makers and program officers. In addition, access to primary schooling is now available to almost 80 percent of all children in the Third World, about double the rate of only thirty years ago. This access has required massive inputs of money, work, and organization and is surely one of the great social achievements of our time.

As a consequence of such large-scale successes, there exists a certain perception that everything possible is being done that can be done to promote children's welfare in the Third World. Of course, there is truth in this viewpoint, since many dedicated people are doing much to improve children's lives. Nevertheless, a number of structural constraints tend to defeat even well-intentioned policy makers. These constraints are familiar to those working in international development and include budgetary limitations, political

Although Harold W. Stevenson was not directly involved in the production of this volume, the editor would like to acknowledge his help. Without his general intellectual and personal support and collaboration over the years, the interdisciplinary direction of this work would have been much less likely. In addition, the Spencer Foundation, the National Institutes of Health (HD-14898), and the National Institute of Education (G-80-0182) provided support in the preparation of this volume.

infighting, and lack of trained personnel. Certain kinds of programs also seem to be more tractable than others: Building a bridge may require less effort than changing attitudes toward birth control; providing better-quality textbooks or new curricula may be easier than knowing how these changes will affect the chances for future employment of the students use them. In short, creating successful social programs means that goods and services not only must reach their intended clientele but also must achieve their intended purposes.

Clearly, in every society some social programs have succeeded and others have failed; but, more commonly, they have succeeded in some respects and failed in others. In the industrialized and highly educated nations, an identifiable component contributing to the success of social programs for children's welfare has been the involvement of social scientists who are knowledgable about children's developmental needs. In large-scale social programs, such as the Head Start program for American children, social scientists and child specialists not only provided expertise for implementation but also testified before Congress as to the program's relevance. In child-oriented programs that involve such domains as health, early education, and literacy, policy makers seldom have the necessary expertise to decide among various options and evaluate the outcomes, but child development researchers can draw on several decades of applied and theoretical work to provide informed advice.

In the Third World, the story is quite different. Social programs have seen only limited success because neither the donor organizations nor the recipient developing countries have sufficient expertise to assess the childhood and societal factors that largely determine the effectiveness of particular social programs. For a number of historical reasons, international organizations primarily employ administrators and accountants to monitor their programs. With their modest finances and compressed schedules, international organizations can devote little time to programs' issues and problems, including careful maintenance and serious evaluation. Likewise, recipient governments usually lack well-trained local child development specialists who are available to work in these programs. The dearth of such specialists is typical throughout the Third World and results, to some extent, from previously established priorities. Indeed, even in Europe and in the United States, the tremendous growth in the numbers of child development and education professionals dates back only a few decades. In addition to this sheer lack of numbers in the Third World, any local people who are trained in child development have usually studied in European or American universities, thereby acquiring a Western perspective that is sometimes at odds with local social and cultural realities.

Children's welfare, like other social concerns, is bound up in everyday political and economic realities. Nevertheless, there is a fair degree of agreement across a wide political spectrum that the welfare of children should encompass such concerns as child health, education, literacy, employment, and lower infant mortality.

Currently available social science knowledge and expertise is too seldom brought to bear on planning and implementation of programs that affect children's lives. It is the purpose of this sourcebook to suggest some new directions for applying such knowledge. First, more collaboration is necessary between international and national organizations and child development specialists in the Third World. Second, efforts should be focused on training local Third World people in child development; concomitantly, greater numbers of Western child development specialists need to become aware of Third World cultures and cross-cultural research strategies. Third, more research on child development in specific Third World cultures must be carried out so that relevant information will be available when it is needed. Finally, human and financial resources are required so that program development and implementation will relate directly to research findings. Regarding this last point, there needs to be greater use of networks among those social scientists and organizations concerned with children's issues. (In fact, existing networks are now being improved; see UNESCO, 1982).

In principle, the clientele of social programs should be the best advocates of governmental or international support. In the case of children—in numbers, the largest of the world's clienteles—such advocacy is obviously impossible. Therefore, the task of providing for children's needs belongs to those who both care and know about children. Establishing a more stable and fluid interface between the currently separate domains of child research and child welfare policy is a crucial and obvious necessity, but requires researchers and planners to depart from old habits. This volume is intended as such as collaborative effort. We hope it will have the support of all those who wish to ensure that collaboration and cross-disciplinary efforts will become more common in research and policy-making circles.

The chapters in this volume address selected child development issues with policy implications for the Third World. (The first five chapters and Chapter Seven were originally presented as papers at a symposium entitled "Child Development and International Development: Research–Policy Interfaces," held in January 1982 as part of the meetings of the American Association for the Advancement of Science.) In addition to chapters on urban migration (Hollnsteiner and Taçon), child survival (Cochrane and Mehra), fertility (LeVine), maternal employment (Engle), literacy (Wagner), and a general discussion (Sutton) presented at the 1982 meetings of the American Association for the Advancement of Science, there is a chapter with an annotated bibliography on child labor (Moore). The final chapter presents a brief summary of resources for additional exploration of the interface between child development and international development.

Far from being comprehensive, this small volume is merely a beginning. It attempts to give impetus to greater collaborative efforts between researchers and policy makers by demonstrating how child development researchers can contribute to an understanding of complex human issues that require policy decisions. Many people recognize the need for such collaboration, but few have been motivated, qualified, or free to begin and maintain this process. With ever increasing expectations of fiscal accountability in social programs, the need for research on promoting effective programs for children has never been greater.

Daniel A. Wagner
Editor

Reference

UNESCO. *Childhood Inequities and Development.* Paris: UNESCO/University of Qatar, 1982.

Daniel A. Wagner is associate professor of human development in the Graduate School of Education, University of Pennsylvania. He is primarily interested in child development in the Third World and is currently involved in a four-year research project on the acquisition and maintenance of literacy in Morocco. With Harold W. Stevenson, he edited Cultural Perspectives on Child Development *(W. H. Freeman, 1982).*

Since urban migration is increasing in the Third World, researchers must turn their efforts toward finding solutions to the many associated problems for families.

Urban Migration in Developing Countries: Consequences for Families and Their Children

Mary Racelis Hollnsteiner
Peter Taçon

Down in the valleys women scratch the soil that is left, and the maize hardly reaches the height of a man. They are valleys of old men and old women, of mothers and children. The men are away, the young men and the girls are away. The soil cannot keep them anymore.
—Alan Paton
Cry, the Beloved Country

* * *

I was born on this pavement spot in front of the airline office fifteen years ago. My parents went to work one day when I was ten and never came back. They left this place to me—a kind of inheritance. My two younger brothers are with me, there under the blanket. We get food sometimes from the people in the airline office. They know we belong here. I run errands for them, like bringing morning tea or running after a customer who has forgotten something. This is a very valuable place. Men have tried to take it but the Sikhs do not let them. The guards also let me help the cleaning women at night. I am very thankful to God for my good fortune.
—Paraphrased from Denis Murphy,
Mother India

Fiction writers often capture the essence of social phenomena better than empirically oriented social scientists do. "The soil cannot keep them anymore" summarizes thousands of scientific observations on the causes of rural-to-urban migration in South Africa and elsewhere. In describing what objectively can be identified only as a life of misery, the young Calcutta girl nevertheless subjectively interprets her circumstances as occasions for gratitude in comparison with the circumstances of other pavement dwellers.

One basic issue in human development is this: An understanding of people's objective circumstances and a respect for their subjective perceptions of life situations must serve as starting points for outside planners and administrators addressing the problems of urban migration. Supplement the people's understanding, wishes, and organized action with sound research and analysis (in which the people should share and to which they should give their own interpretations) of the social, political, economic and other factors that create and intensify problems, add the political will needed to achieve institutional and technological breakthroughs, and one has the makings of real solutions.

Urbanization and Migration Trends

What are the forces that transform children into children of migrant families—the subject of our concern here? Urbanization is one such force. Beginning some 10,000 years ago in Sumer, urbanization picked up speed in the sixteenth and seventeenth centuries, when the world urban population hovered between 1 and 2 percent; accelerated still more in industrializing eighteenth, nineteenth, and early twentieth-century England, Western Europe, and later North America; rose even faster in Latin America and North Africa by the mid-twentieth century; and subsequently increased in Asia and sub-saharan Africa. There is reason to expect a virtually 100 percent urban world by the year 2100 (Davis, 1972, pp. 17, 121, 129). The last quarter of this century promises extraordinarily rapid rises in developing-country urban populations: in Africa, 336 percent, in South Asia, 298 percent, in Latin America, 235 percent, and in East Asia (excluding Japan), 225 percent, contrasted with the industrialized regions at 42 percent (United Nations, 1980).

Estimates indicate a predominantly urban world by the year 2000 (61.5 percent), with a global urban population ranging from 3.2 to 3.9 billion. Two thirds will be located in developing countries, and the other third in the industrialized countries (United Nations, 1980). The sheer magnitude of developing-country urban populations will place over 2 billion people— and almost three quarters of a billion children up to the age of fourteen—in developing-country cities and towns (see Figure 1). Cities all over the world with populations of a million or more will claim some 1.74 billion residents, with medium (500,000 and over), and small-sized (100,000 and over) cities similarly drawing huge numbers (Davis, 1972, pp. 17, 121, 129). Twenty-first

Figure 1. Total and Child Population in Urban Areas in All Less-Developed Regions, 1975-2000

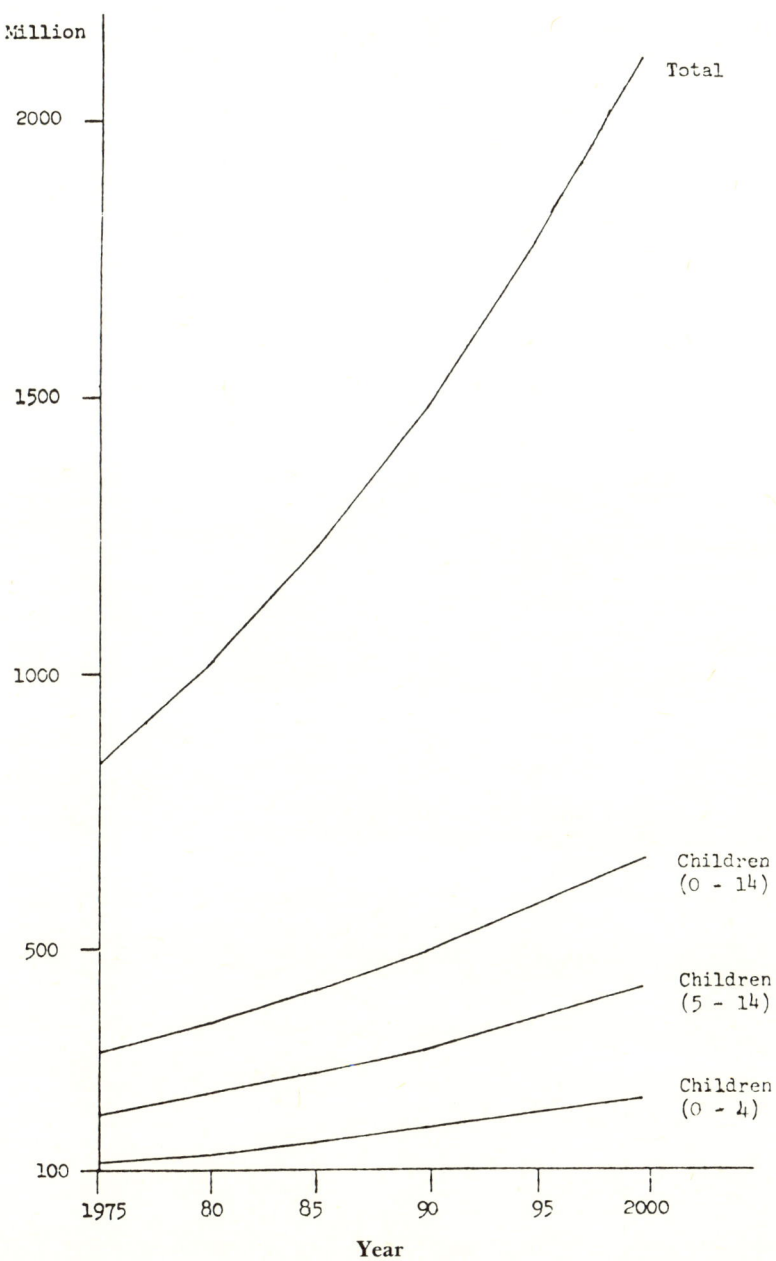

Source: United Nations Population Division, 1981.

century urban children will thus be predominantly city dwellers, rather than town dwellers, with the heaviest concentrations in Middle South Asia, China, and Latin America (See Figure 2). Moreover, if trends of the 1960s and the 1970s persist, from 17 to 70 percent of the urban population will be squatters and slum dwellers, the majority of them children, with all the deprivation and insecurity that status implies (see Table 1) (Laquian, 1980, p. 149).

Although the massive migrations from countryside to cities would appear to be the prime cause of rapid urban growth in developing countries, the data contradict this assumption. Rather, developing-country urban growth stems largely from high rates of natural population increase, with an average of 60.7 percent of urban populations being attributable to this source,

Table 1. Extent of Squatting and Slum Dwelling in Selected Cities

Region and City	Year	City Population (in thousands)	Slum Dwellers and Squatters	Percentage of Slum Dwellers and Squatters to City Population
Africa				
Casablanca	1971	1,506	1,054	70
Kinshasa	1969	1,288	733	60
Nairobi	1970	535	177	33
South Asia				
Calcutta	1971	8,000	5,328	67
Bombay	1971	6,000	2,475	41
Delhi	1970	3,877	1,400	36
Dacca	1973	1,700	300	35
Karachi	1971	3,428	800	23
Latin America				
Bogota	1969	2,294	1,376	60
Buenos Aires	1970	2,972	1,468	50
Mexico City	1966	3,287	1,500	46
Caracas	1974	2,369	1,000	42
Lima	1970	2,877	1,148	40
Rio de Janeiro	1970	4,855	1,456	30
Santiago	1964	2,184	546	25
East Asia				
Manila	1972	4,400	1,540	35
Pusan	1969	1,675	527	31
Seoul	1969	4,600	1,320	29
Jakarta	1972	4,576	1,190	26
Bangkok/ Thonburi	1970	3,041	600	20
Hong Kong	1969	3,617	600	17
Europe				
Ankara	1970	1,250	750	60
Istanbul	1970	2,247	899	40

Source: United Nations Housing Survey (1976) and IDRC (1979), quoted in Laquian (1980).

Figure 2. Proportion of All Urban Children of Less-Developed Regions in Each Region, 1975-2000

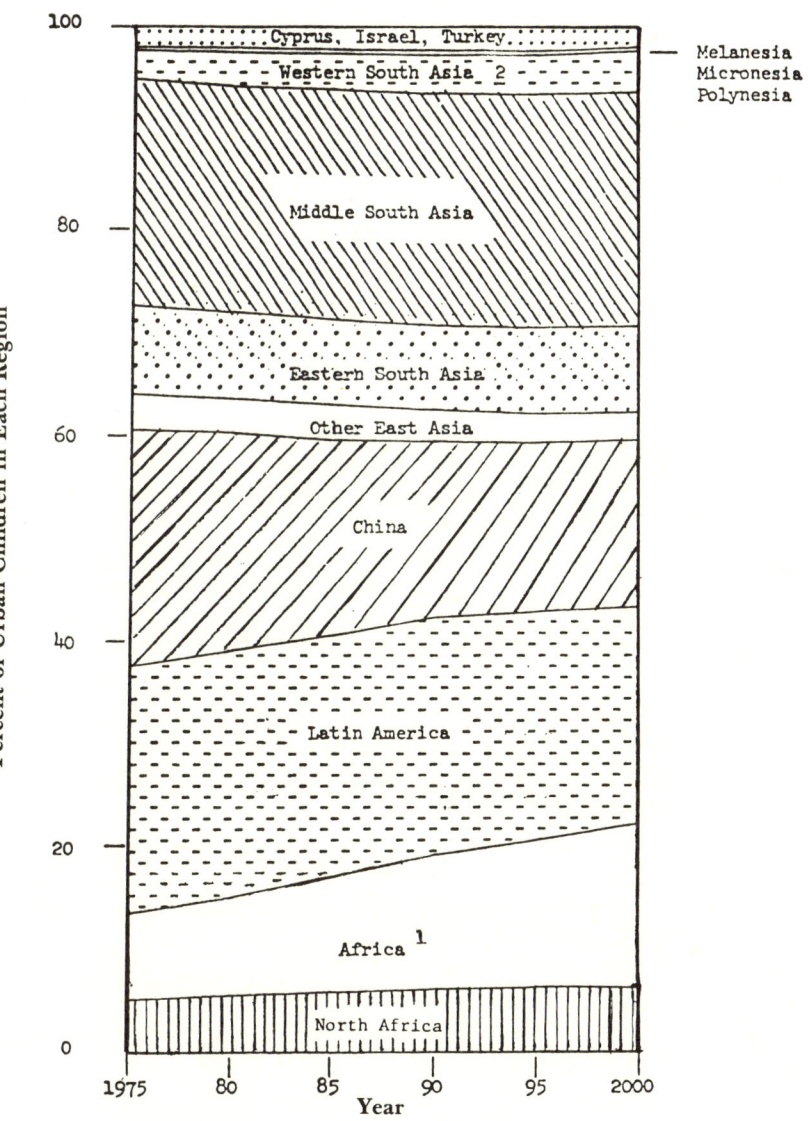

[1] Excluding North Africa
[2] Excluding Cyprus, Israel, and Turkey

Source: United Nations Children's Fund, "Urban Basic Services: Reaching Children and Women of the Urban Poor." Report by the executive director. Executive Board 1982, no. E/ECEF/L.1440, 5 Mar. 1982.

compared with only 39.3 percent for migration. The reverse holds true for industrial countries (40.2 percent for natural increase and 59.8 percent for migration). Only in developing countries that show rapid economic growth (for example, Argentina and the Republic of Korea) does net rural-urban migration contribute to more than half of urban growth. For the majority of countries, where economic growth is slower, natural increase of urban populations themselves probably accounts for two thirds of urban increments (United Nations, 1980, p. 11).

The proportion of migrant entries may be relatively small in developing countries vis-à-vis urban births, but the absolute number of people represented by these percentages is staggering. They leave their rural homes for a variety of reasons: the promise of economic opportunities and a better future in the cities, coupled with the deterioration of rural sources of livelihood; the availability of social services, like health care and education, in urban areas; the relative flexibility accorded the behavior and values of urbanites in modern environments versus strictures on peasants in largely traditional environments; the attractions of faster-paced modern life and of technology; and the physical insecurity in rural areas stemming from lawlessness, banditry, incipient revolutionary movements, and other kinds of social unrest (United Nations, 1968, pp. 91-92).

For rural children, migration means one or more types of adjustments. They are left behind with their mothers, while their fathers go off to look for work in towns or cities. If they extend their urban stays, fathers may send for their families or visit them sporadically or, sometimes, end up abandoning them. If those fathers are among those considered lucky enough to have joined the international migration stream (usually a pool of skilled or semiskilled labor destined for the Middle East or Europe), they probably remit enough funds to improve their families' level of living. Whether the families' economic fortunes increase, decrease, or remain unchanged, however, the absence of fathers can produce serious strains. Mothers are hard pressed when they are unaccustomed to making agricultural decisions or when they lack the skills to manage areas generally considered to be in the male domain. They can turn to their kinfolk for help, but these relatives may not be eager to help if they are beset with problems of their own. Children are conscripted into the household farm, fishing, or pastoral labor force to make up for their fathers' absence and for the resulting labor deficit, which is often exacerbated by the move of older sisters to the city. Other children must become full-time caretakers for their younger siblings. School attendance declines correspondingly. Similarly, the mother who must spend more time on her absent husband's tasks gives less time to her younger children than would be the case if he were present. These complications are compounded when a migrant father fails to send money back to his family. This lapse may stem from circumstances (inability to find work, the father's gambling, or drinking) or may be by design, as when he moves in with another woman and starts a second family in the city.

A second major migration pattern has both parents moving with their children to the city. Possibly, one or both parents have visited there frequently enough to have made a reasonably accurate assessment of opportunities and to have established kin or friendship linkages. Alternatively, the family may brave uncertainty and sally forth trusting to luck, God, or other supernatural supports. In either case, the children of these migrant families are likely to suffer the most, recent arrivals being especially vulnerable to illness and even death. Youngsters in the third category of migrant children—those born in the city or the town to which their parents have migrated—suffer similar kinds of deprivation.

Children in Urban Slums and Squatter Areas

Multiple Adversities. Whether they are born in the countryside or in the city, stress becomes a regular feature of poor migrant children's lives, transmitted as it is through families beset by multiple adversities:

> When rural people first reach the city they are frequently at a social, psychological, economic, and physical disadvantage. They are entering a new social milieu with different norms, living modes, and institutions. Often they confront this new environment with little support from their traditional social structure. Their education and skill levels are generally low and their familiarity with the job market limited, with the result that they have difficulty finding long-term employment. They are forced to live in generally crowded and poor-quality housing. Clinically they may carry diseases unfamiliar to the regions into which they have migrated.... Some ethnic groups and caste groups within ethnic groups will be discriminated against across the board, so that they will live in inferior housing in sections of the town with inferior services of all kinds and will have unusually high unemployment rates [Austin, 1976, pp. 5, 7, 17, 19].

Malnutrition, Poor Health, and Infant Mortality. The most immediate and acute effects of urban poverty on children are malnutrition and poor health. The caloric intake of urban dwellers is frequently lower than that of their rural counterparts. The World Bank lists 362 million urban poor people suffering from calorie deficits, of whom 119 million infants, young children, pregnant women, and nursing mothers fall into the undernourished and severely undernourished vulnerable subgroup. A Harvard team investigating urban malnutrition dramatized the situation this way:

> What do these numbers mean? First and foremost they mean deprivation and human suffering on an awesome scale. The humanitarian necessity for alleviation is obvious, but the justification for act-

ing goes beyond this. The numbers suggest the possibility of serious erosion of human capital, which in turn could seriously impede the development process from both growth and equity perspectives. The erosion can occur along the mental and physical dimensions. Severe malnutrition can cause serious retardation in brain development. Less severe malnutrition may reduce parent and child energy levels so that listlessness becomes the norm; the social stimulation essential to cognitive development is absent and mental potential goes unrealized. Physical work capacity can be reduced, for example, by calorie or iron deficiencies or, additionally, by vitamin A deficiency, which impairs vision and can cause blindness.

Poor nutrition increases disease susceptibility and thus contributes to lost work days due either to parent sickness or to increased parent–child care time, due to child illness. The large number of infant deaths due directly or indirectly to malnutrition eliminates future work force members and their expected economic contribution. The loss of children also imposes emotional and time-draining burdens on parents; these undoubtedly carry negative effects on their short-run productivity. Furthermore, malnutrition carries significant negative externalities for other development investments. Programs aimed at stimulating self-help and community development are severely handicapped if people have barely enough physical and psychic energy to carry out their normal work and family duties, let alone undertake additional communal tasks. Children who enter school having already incurred or even suffering the adverse mental development effects of malnutrition are not in a position to fully gain the potential benefits of education, thereby reducing the return to society of existing investment in education intrastructures. Finally, the higher incidence and severity of illness due to poor nutritional status adds to society's health care burden, either by increasing the funds needed for health facilities or by overburdening the existing services and decreasing their effectiveness [Austin and others, 1976, pp. 5, 7, 17, 19].

Malnutrition victimizes poor urban children earlier in their lives than it does rural children. The single greatest reason for this trend is the growing tendency of the urban mother to bottle-feed instead of breastfeeding her baby. Several factors account for this decision—the mother's need to join in the household quest for additional income by working outside the home in places with no crêche facilities; her exposure to hospital practices that separate mother and newborn and that initiate bottle-feeding, with the encouragement of commercial infant-formula manufacturers; and an image of "modernity" and "health" fostered by infant-formula advertising.

The absence of breastfeeding deprives an infant of naturally built-in immunities against illnesses. Moreover, by resorting to bottle-feeding, a poor mother exposes her child to serious infection and diarrhea engendered by contaminated water, dirty bottles, and re-use of leftover commerical formula. Although statistics on infant mortality show higher rates for rural than for urban babies, the urban figures are misleading, since they include better-off infants from upper- and middle-class families. Few studies are available in the developing countries that disaggregate urban infant mortality rates by class or slum and squatter residential status. A five-year study (1969-1974) of poor slum neighborhoods in Kanpur, Uttar Pradesh (India), revealed a devastatingly high infant mortality rate of 454 per 1,000. This rate contrasts with 80 infant deaths per 1,000 for urban India as a whole, and 139 per 1,000 for rural India (Sandell and Sandell, 1981).

Even if infants survive the neonatal period, they face added dangers from about the fourth month on, when they should be receiving supplementary weaning food. In fact, if the neonatal period is excluded, second-year infant mortality rates often turn out to be higher than the first-year rates. This circumstance is largely the result of insufficient food intake and the dangerous tendency of uneducated mothers unwittingly to bring on dehydration in diarrheal infants by depriving them of liquids. The education of women makes a difference in child survival. A case in point is India, where the infant mortality rate among children of illiterate mothers stands at 81 per 1,000, in contrast to 59 per 1,000 where mothers have had some primary education and 49 per 1,000 where mothers have completed at least primary education. Similar associations have been made in India between lowered infant mortality rates and the presence of urban amenities like safe drinking water, primary schools, and medical facilities (see Table 2) (UNICEF, 1981, p. 35).

Anxieties of Moving. For urban migrant children, reaching their first homes in the city is the start of a series of moves they and their families are likely to make over the next decade. A 1975 study of low-income migrant families in one district of Manila, Philippines, revealed that nine out of ten household heads, singly or with their families, had moved from one residence to another within a few years of arriving in the city. Multiple reasons were given: eviction, especially for the squatter families; high rents and the search for cheaper dwellings; a desire to be near one's workplace, for convenience and to cut down on transportation costs; marriage and the formation of a new household unit; a preference for living with relatives and in-laws or, conversely, the

Table 2. Infant Mortality Rates (IMR) in Urban India Classified According to Presence or Absence of Selected Basic Services

Type of Basic Service	IMR with Basic Services	IMR Without Basic Services
Safe drinking water	66	94
Primary school	65	71
Medical facilities	57	71

desire to move away from them; buying one's own house; and disasters like floods or fires (Hollnsteiner and Lopez, 1976). Whatever the reason, migrant children must face the difficulties of making new friends, trying to get into other schools, or, in the case of infants, having to readapt to their mothers' new work or activity schedules. For squatter children, in particular, moving may mean yet another miserable shack in a worse environment, thrown together from the remains of structures torn down earlier by evicting authorities and now, as a result, smaller and more crowded.

Education as a Privilege. The rural families who migrate to cities in the hope that their children will gain access to better education often find their dreams dashed by an unsympathetic educational establishment. Harrassed administrators in overcrowded schools turn newcomers away as ineligible because they have not established bona fide residence in the neighborhood or because, being squatters, their tenure in the city is illegal. Kun Prateep, a dedicated Thai leader in Klong Toey, one of the two largest squatter areas in Southeast Asia, tells her story: "In our slum, as well as in other slums in Bangkok, many of the inhabitants do not have house registration numbers and some families have no identity cards. Without these vital papers parents cannot obtain birth certificates for their children and without a birth certificate a child cannot enroll in a school. Consequently, many children in the slums grow up without any chance of learning to read or write" (Ungsongtham, 1977, pp. 13-14). Although a district officer subsequently gave special approval for children without identification cards or birth certificates to apply for them, parents were apprehensive about being fined if they did apply. Eventually, even this concession was eliminated, when government representatives said they could not risk giving identity cards to (non-Thai) aliens who might infiltrate the slums and, pretending to be residents, claim identity cards.

Slum children encounter other blocks to acquiring basic education. Parents may feel education is not worth the time, especially for girls, and may prefer that their children spend their time in income-generating activities. Again, older children may have to watch their younger siblings during the day while both parents are out working. Still other children lose interest in school and voluntarily drop out when they are mixed with economically better-off children and are jeered at for their tattered clothing, unkempt and dirty appearance, and foul smell. The scarcity of water in their neighborhoods prevents regular bathing, while the sheer pressure of their parents' long work hours allows little time for grooming the children. The result is that if these children do go to school, many of them are sulky, moody, and withdrawn and refuse to answer questions. Many are also drowsy after working well into the night as minibus ticket collectors or collecting waste fats thrown out by the nearby slaughter house; others are both tired and hungry, not having had breakfast before school (Ungsongtham, 1977, pp. 13-14).

Another kind of nurturing and learning experience rarely available to poor urban infants and young children under six years of age are crêches and preschool nursery-kindergartens. While many children have relatives or concerned neighbors nearby who see to their safety and feeding while the parents are at work, others have to rely solely on older siblings, some of them only nine or ten years old. Among the poorest groups in India, large numbers of itinerant ragpickers, coal gatherers, and unskilled construction laborers are women. Their children accompany them to the worksites, prompting the observation that "for centuries this child has lain by the roadside while his parents build magnificent cities. When you pass by a bundle of rags you do not realize that there is a baby inside until you hear it cry" (Mahadevan, 1977, pp. 26–27). The energetic group of Indian women who founded mobile crèches to address this problem opted for simple enclosed centers right on the worksites. They followed the tradition of beautifying simple huts or rooms by using the appropriate indigenous material: "The equipment was also simple and familiar to the mothers. For example, the cradle that we use in our crèches is typically Indian and versatile. Throughout rural India this kind of cradle is used and it costs next to nothing. The cloth hammock in which the baby sleeps is easy to wash. "The accommodation allotted to us is usually drab. It may be housed in a basement or on the eighteenth floor of an unfinished skyscraper. With the work going on in full swing around us and dust floating, we do our best to keep the place pleasant. To mellow down the harsh surrounding, the workers decorate the place with the children's colorful drawings. The cradles and cots of the babies have lovely mobiles hanging on them" (Mahadevan, 1977, pp. 26–27).

Learning activities, especially for the four- to six-year-olds, center around storytelling and folk tales worked into nursery rhymes. Aside from providing basic care and many other services, these mobile crèches offer the early stimulation so essential to young children's cognitive, intellectual, and motor development. Yet, despite the enthusiasm with which most parents welcome and cooperate with these attempts to provide a safe, stimulating, and organized play environment for their young children, rare is the city government that promotes, much less initiates, such important activities.

Children Without Families: The Latin American Case

Perhaps the greatest victims of rapid urban migration are the millions of children and adolescents up to seventeen years old (the age of majority) who have been deprived of the material and moral support, affection, and protection of their natural families. Their circumstances of life do not allow them the two basic elements that families provide: (1) at least one person who will nurture and defend them and (2) an identity (Taçon, 1981a). In thinking about children without families, "we must consider not only the materially abandoned child cast into the streets absolutely, but the neglected child who lives most of his life on city streets abandoned de facto, the abused child who has lost any 'identity partner' within his own family, the exploited child who must work often under intolerable conditions to bring home his 'daily quota' to help support what is almost always a fatherless family group, and the morally abandoned child (most noticeable in northern developed countries) who may have everything he or she requires materially but lacks a home even though he or she has a house. We must also consider the child who, because of abuse, neglect, exploitation, or (as is so frequent in developing countries) extreme poverty, chooses himself or herself to leave the family unit, seeking relief and a better chance of survival on the streets. We must be particularly concerned with the child who all too often encounters extreme violence as a cause of and/or as a result of his loss or family and thus abandonment" (Taçon, 1981b, pp. 9–12).

Although the numbers of children in this category are difficult to ascertain, estimates suggest that there are some 70 million fully or partly abandoned and street children in developing countries—40 million in Latin America and the Caribbean, 20 million in Asia, and 10 million in Africa. Another 10 million morally abandoned children are estimated in developed countries.

There are approximately 400 million people living in Latin America and the Caribbean today, of whom roughly 200 million are children are under the age of eighteen years. More than half of this total population of 400 million lives in cities, and that number grows dramatically day by day. In Mexico City, 1,500 rural-to-urban migrants arrive daily. During the past forty years in Brazil, the percentage of the population living in cities has increased from 30 percent to nearly 70 percent, and well over half of those 90 million city dwellers live in urban slum environments.

Of this region's 200 million children, it is calculated that at least 40 million live in such crisis-ridden families that they can be considered either totally or de facto abandoned. Something on the order of 25 million of these children live in Brazil alone. Information from government and private authorities suggests that between 70 and 80 percent of these children come either from mother-only families or from families in which the adult male is not the natural father but, rather, is one of a series of partners of the children's natural mother. All the above statistics proclaim the very serious state of this region's children, the critical extent of family disintegration, the high levels of human tension and insecurity that accompany extreme poverty, and the instability of life itself. The street children who are spawned by this poverty and instability may lead very different lives in Bogotá, São Paula, or Guadalajara—forced to beg, steal, prostitute themselves, and trade off abuse and exploitation for survival—but they all have one thing in common. The "industrial miracle" that is so often associated with at least part of the Latin American region has touched their lives dramatically—but with oppression and not promise, with denial and not benefit. These 40 million street children represent the most painful byproduct of economic progress, in which they and their parents are not allowed to participate, save with the sacrifice of human dignity and life itself.

A Move to the City. It is highly likely that, at this very moment, more than a million poor rural families in Latin America are making the decision to move, to seek what they have decided must be the better, urban life. They are looking for a way out of the tedious struggle for subsistence, of working land that probably belongs to someone else, or of having had their services and skills replaced by a tractor or other agents of agricultural mechanization. In the city, they see hope for educating their children, water that arrives clean to the house, easy access to markets and good food, neighbors, and a sense of community. They are tired of the simple life on the farm, which leads nowhere and is often bearable only because of the proximity of the extended family. They find the chance of participating in the surging activity of city life compelling and they will flee the countryside someday soon to become part of the new promise for the future, which comes to them daily via their transistor radios. Many of these families will move directly to a national or a state capital, but others will move progressively from smaller towns to larger ones until, like the others, they reach the outskirts of the great metropolitan cities. They will leave behind traditional family ties (and the security these hold for their children in case the parents die), and they will be forced to forsake many of the cultural values that have guided them so constantly through life. For better or for worse, each family will be almost entirely on its own. Together, they will move upon the slums that encircle the major centers of population. They will be like an army of Quixotes, poorly trained and ill equipped to do battle with the unyielding windmills of urban insensitivity. Perhaps half those hopeful migrant families, and maybe more, will succeed in their newfound city homes. Perhaps, too, the move they are about to make will produce another million or more street children.

It is common that families who migrate to the cities of Latin America find themselves exchanging the "clean" poverty they had in the country for the "dirty" poverty of urban slums. Moving first into transient shantytowns, they will try to establish a more permanent home in the years ahead, if conditions permit. They become squatters or invaders of whatever land is available, whether it is owned privately or by local government. To add to the insecurity of their tenure and the precarious nature of their housing, these new urban residents will encounter, perhaps for many years to come, serious problems involving clean water accessibility, sewage, sanitation, health care, education services, fuel, electricity, and transportation. Their most serious long-term problems, however, will be employment and income generation.

In the beginning, new arrivals from the country may feel a sense of togetherness and a pioneering spirit, but the frustrations that arise from being unable to resolve even the most basic problems for family well-being soon will dispel the novelty of city life. Initial feelings of solidarity within the new community are forced to give way to each family's independent quest for survival. Very frequently, continuing stress on the family will result in the departure of the father: "¡*Yo no valgo!*" he exclaims ("I am worthless"), leaving the abandoned mother in what is too often the virtually impossible situation of trying, without resources, to arrange the survival of her children and herself. As one of millions of women in Latin America who have suffered continuing discrimination since birth—for having been born female—she has received little if any formal education and is likely to be completely illiterate. Trained for little else than domestic servitude and dedication to her children, she has been taught that a woman cannot be anything but an appendage to a man. Now, she is suddenly faced with the grim reality of trying to support a young and growing family of perhaps four, five, or more children of varying ages and of limited capacities to help her. She may have to work outside the home (most likely in street selling, domestic service, or other forms of subemployment) and leave her older children to care for the younger ones. Alternatively, she must find another man whose earning capacity will allow the family to function from day to day and survive. Yet another possibility is to send the older children out to work or beg on the streets, to return home only when they have managed somehow to earn their quotas of family support. Neither she nor her sons and daughters are equipped to generate more than minimal income; they all can expect hunger and disease to become a pattern of living if another male partner (stepfather) is not found soon. Very often, too, even if such a man does appear on the scene, he is hardly willing to consider these children of another man as his own. Not uncommonly, physical or sexual abuse coupled with exploitation lead children to run away from home rather than face this continuing oppressive onslaught, which could ruin their lives and their mother's new "marriage." Although women do not willingly allow this to happen, they, too, driven by frustration and utter exhaustion, eventually give up. They settle for trying to maintain life for the youngest of five, six, seven, or more youngsters, while the older ones, often as young as seven, leave home to fend for themselves on the street. Girls as well as boys are caught in this painful dilemma, which eventually brings about their abandonment and subsequent destitution in city streets. Because the girls are able to "hire out" as domestics or prostitutes, they are less visible than the boys.

Searching for Prevention. In the Latin American region today, few programs exist to help abandoned mothers keep their families together, and those that do exist for children who face abandonment almost always attempt to attack the problem, whatever it is, after it already exists. The institutionalization of poor children simply because they are poor is commonplace, even though their support frequently costs more per child that it would cost to support an entire original family with a community context. Such curative programs for child abandonment are not only costly but also frequently counterproductive: Preparation of interned children for normal integrated adult community life is always highly complex, if not impossible, and does nothing to save the family as an integral part of society.

To prevent the abandonment of women and children, the abandonment of communities and families must also be prevented. Long before the stresses of urban slum survival cause family breakup, problems must be attacked at their source. Rural development programs must improve the quality of life in the country if the tide of migration to the city is to be stemmed. Immediate legalization of existing urban squatter slums is critically important — with the full participation of squatters themselves — together with the provision of basic health care, sanitation, education, water, and electrical services. Official attitudes, which commonly view the poorest of the poor with indifference or even with hostility, will have to give way to cooperative efforts so that people can help themselves. If communities are to develop the sort of solidarity and conscious awareness that will let them work for a common well-being and protect other families, they must sense hope and the trust of others and receive the resources to which they are entitled (without receiving other imposed conditions, which they do not deserve). They will need both technical and material support, to be sure, but they will not need to be controlled from beyond or from above. Eventually, in fact, even without such assistance, the poor can and will receive justice instead of charity, respect instead of paternalism, dignity instead of repression: In Latin America, it is simply a question of what road revolution will take, not whether it will happen. Will it be the peaceful road that Costa Rica chose in 1948, or will revolution be fought for violently as in Nicaragua thirty years later? The choice depends largely on how the urban poor — including many migrants from rural areas — are treated: as friends, or as enemies. They will respond in kind and with a loud voice.

Signs of Hope. The church and other nongovernmental organizations in Latin America are commonly viewed as the natural allies of the poor and as really dedicated to improving the quality of life, especially in urban slums. A recent on-site evaluation of ten Latin American countries, however, disclosed a number of government initiatives that also provide cause for hope. The National Program of Integrated Family Services (Mexico), the National Board of Family Welfare (Honduras), the National Council of the Child (Dominican Republic), the Colombian Institute for Family Welfare, the Child Welfare Council of Costa Rica, and even the Salvadoran Council of the Child (amidst all the turbulence of that troubled land) are each developing new national programs to reach out to and help, as partners rather than as directors, poor urban communities. Most of these initiatives involve working directly with street children, through whom direct access is gained to the entire family of each child and, through that family, to others in the local community. Regardless of their motivations, these are important new beginnings, which recognize not only the tremendous problems faced by poor urban families but also the possibility of preventive solutions within communities.

Among programs of assistance to mother-only families and to abandoned children (reintegrating them into their own families or finding new families for them), none seems quite so effective as the one now being carried out by the Ministry of Social Welfare of Nicaragua. Perhaps even more impressive was what happened in that country (and is still happening, to a large extent) immediately following the end of the national war there in July 1979. In August of that year, an evaluation team concluded that approximately 70,000 Nicaraguan children were living without family support. By February of 1980, a parallel follow-up study showed that this number had decreased by at least 45,000 — without any official government program at all. According to a local council member in the battered city of Esteli, "We were determined that not one of our children would have to leave us and that not one of our children would be without a family. All of us in Esteli are each child's family." That was a statement of community solidarity that continues to be made. It shows what communities can do when they are mobilized truly to care for their young. Beyond this less formal expression of community togetherness, local programs of income generation through cooperatives for single and abandoned mothers have enjoyed growing success. Children without families are placed either in new foster families or for adoption nationally — not in institutions. In sum, national policy for families is rooted in the Nicaraguan communities.

In Brazil, there has been a new response to the problems of the vast numbers of street children. With what is probably the most serious youth crisis in Latin America, the present government of Brazil is eager to reduce the losses suffered by these girls and boys and by the nation as a whole. A team of representatives from the Ministry of Social Welfare, the National Child Welfare Foundation, and UNICEF is currently working to identify good local private and governmental programs that are truly effective in working with street children at the community level and in working with the direct participation of whole communities. These represent people-centered alternatives to traditional approaches, including institutionalization. Building on these successful projects, the team hopes to teach other communities to develop their own special programs as well as to mobilize nationally the technical and material resources to support these important local initiatives. It is hoped that the principles and the methodology of these community programs of prevention can be incorporated into future national policy, which eventually will result in ending the exploitation of street children and the need for child institutionalization. Once a community decides that not one of its children will be left destitute, there remains no need for expensive curative programs, which so often vainly try to repair damage that need not have been done in the first place.

Latin America: A Harbinger? Urban misery knows no culture; rather, it destroys it. As Asian and African developing countries become more industrialized, they, like Latin American nations, will have to face the culture-threatening effects on families of urbanization and rural-to-urban migration. Today, Asians say with pride that child abandonment is rare because the traditional extended family remains intact; Africans also state that it is unthinkable for a tribe, a community, or a family to permit a child to be abandoned; and yet what is happening today in Bangkok, Nairobi, and a hundred other industrializing cities sounds a cry for help. The picture painted in Seoul, Jakarta, Calcutta, Cairo, and Lagos is becoming not so unlike that in Lima, Caracas, Tijuana, Rio de Janeiro, or Tegucigalpa.

Latin America today is extremely valuable territory for our learning not only about ourselves but also about our neighbors and what can happen to cultures and to people when they and their natural resources become drawn into the kind of industrial "progress" that benefits only a small portion of the populace. Contrary to what many current political observers claim, the fight in Latin America is not for the survival of democracy or of capitalism; the real fight in this sadly neglected region of our world is for the survival of the family as an institution and of children without families as truly human beings.

The Paradoxical Attraction of Urban Slums

Highlighting the negative impact of slums on migrant children is necessary for identifying the multiple problems that enlightened urban leadership must address. At the same time, we should recognize that millions of migrant parents would not choose urban life unless it offered a significant number of redeeming features. No matter how wretched their housing and environmental conditions, how insecure their residential tenure, how uncertain or undesirable their employment, or how disturbed their family relationships, migrant parents either feel the risk is worth taking or simply accept the reality that their former, rural way of life is no longer possible. The city can be a place of hope for many, of permanent despair and degradation for others. For the more fortunate, despair and degradation turn out to be only temporary states in the search for a meaningful place in the city.

Attractions that counteract the deficiencies of the slums and the shantytowns come in many forms. A sense of community reminiscent of village life persists in many urban neighborhood clusters and is fostered by social as well as economic necessity in the face of unresponsive urban institutions and by sheer tradition. The same population density that breeds quarrels and fights among neighbors also encourages helpful relationships. Living in the vicinity of one's transplanted ethnic or language group, caste, or occupation group allows bonds of reciprocal service and friendship to flourish.

Low-income neighborhood residence also provides a means of upward mobility. Significant features are low rents; information from kin, friends, and neighbors on how to manage in the city; and the possibility of inserting oneself somewhere in the informal urban-services–oriented economy while awaiting a more stable job. Although employment conditions are poor and incomes low, comparisons in most developing countries show that, on the whole, poor urban residents in the informal economy earn more than their rural counterparts. Similarly, while urban services and amenities like health care, education, and housing remain far from adequate, they still are more readily available to city dwellers than to their country kinfolk. From a relative perspective, then, in which migrant families subjectively compare their present and future prospects with those of their rural neighbors, urban residence offers more advantages.

The tolerance of slum dwellers for minimal amenities and services cannot, however, be used by administrators and planners as an excuse for ignoring the needs of the urban poor. Not only are they citizens with a right to decent levels of living; they also represent human resources whose capacities for contributing to society are enormous, if given a chance. Conversely, frustrated and angry urban populations, if too long denied, can generate conflict and disorder through mass protests, strikes, terrorism, and urban guerrilla warfare.

The Research–Policy Interface

Strategies for People-Oriented Policies. The solutions to urban poverty, and to the migration that is so much a part of it, lie basically in structural reform of the societies that still favor elite minority interests over the welfare of the striving majority. The means of achieving this transformation have been discussed in many other writings and are too complex for discussion here. For the city and community levels, however, certain changes must be effected if the well-being of the residents is taken seriously.

The sine qua non of any urban development activity to benefit the poor is their participation in the decision-making processes affecting their situation. This participation entails their help to identify problems, establish priorities, determine the actions to be taken, implement and monitor these actions, and evaluate overall strategies and techniques before determining the next moves. Organized groups do this most effectively; yet, because violent protests gain the greatest publicity, many urban administrators fear popular participation, since they mistakenly assume that it aims at overthrowing the city administration, if not the government as a whole. In reality, violence represents the exception rather than the rule. A sample of 545 migrants in Mexico City, for example listed their preferred strategies of demand making as follows (Cornelius, 1975, p. 13):

Strategy	Percent
Sending a representative to a government office	47.9
Working through personal connections with public officials	25.2
Working through the official party	11.5
Organizing a protest demonstration	9.5
Organizing public meetings or rallies to get other people interested in the problem	5.8

Furthermore, as a squatter leader in Manila's Tondo Foreshore once exclaimed, "Why do the housing authority leaders and the military always jump to the conclusion that we are trying to overthrow the system, when all we want to do is get *into* the system?"

While hunger is surely the most pressing issue, worried parents recognize that, without a firmer foothold in the city, feeding their families will be a never-ending problem. For migrants and squatters consistently threatened with eviction—whether in Klong Toey, the Tondo Foreshore, Kanpur, or Colonia Perifírico in Mexico City—security of residential tenure constitutes their most important perceived need. Of the 112 migrants surveyed in Mexico City *colonias,* 65 percent listed security of tenure as the subject they most often brought to government officials' attention. The next subject drew far fewer mentions—water supply (11 percent). The rest of the issues garnered only 1 to 8 percent of the total responses (postal service, street pavement, personal or family-related problems, electricity, schools, public transportation, sewage, garbage collection, and other community-related problems; see Cornelius, 1975, p. 13). Housing is not even mentioned, yet it is the amenity most often thought by urban officials to be most significant, perhaps because it is the most obvious problem that can be seen from the outside. As far as migrants and squatters are concerned, however, improved housing can wait and be subjected to gradual upgrading until land and employment are more assured.

It goes without saying that employment opportunities, skills training, and financial credit constitute crucial inputs to rising levels of living and effective mechanism for coping with urban life. Programs aimed at improving urban social services that the people themselves can manage, together with city government that is sympathetic, responsive, and flexible in its procedures, can go far to alleviate the dire conditions of poor children (Cousins and Goyder, 1979).

Existing efforts to address the special problems of abandoned or street children need to be expanded, disseminated, replicated, and adapted to local circumstances. These approaches stress the importance of solid community involvement, in which members see all children as their own and where families can act as the children's new identity partners. This is part of the process of reintegrating children into warm and loving family environments—either the reconstructed natural family, an extended kinship system, or a creative family alternative. Attention should also go to the preventive strategy of attacking problems at their source (Taçon, 1981a, p. 1; 1981b, pp. 9-12).

Educating women; helping them generate income through credit schemes, skills, and management training; still enabling them to give their children proper care through community-based crêche arrangements; making appropriate technology available to reduce their household workload and increase their work efficiency—all these steps will benefit not only women but also other household members, most especially children. Studies in various parts of the developing world reveal that mothers who earn and control their incomes devote the bulk of it to the welfare of their children, in contrast to fathers' allocations for their families. Men do have to spend a part of their incomes for housing, transportation, and other such expenses, but tend in many instances also to spend inordinate amounts on drinking, gambling, and other women. When the poorest men have more than one family to support, abandonment of at least one of the families is common. Thus, developmental programs focused on women are even more urgent, especially when women are the sole support of children. The global average for women-headed households in developing countries is about 18 percent. In some parts of the world, the figure is much higher; the Caribbean is a case in point, with some 60 percent of households reported to be headed by women, most of them poor (Buvinic, Youssef, and Von Elm, 1978).

Research for and with People. What are the implications for research priorities? High on the list should be clearer understanding of the global and national macrosystems that generate the structures and behaviors conducive both to massive migration and to slum and squatter conditions for millions of Third World urban families. Applied research, focusing on the concrete social problems of poverty and deprivation and on ways of addressing them effectively, can no longer be regarded as lower in status than the "purer" kinds of basic research still favored by many university establishments. Collection and presentation of statistics on urban populations should disaggregate the urban poor from urban populations as a whole, migrants from nonmigrants, children in slums and squatter areas from their better-off counterparts, poor children without families from those with families, and other significant problem-oriented distinctions. By joining with action groups tackling problems of migrant adaptation, family stress, disadvantaged children, and a host of other concerns, social scientists will be able to bring the tools of their disciplines to the service of the most vulnerable, even as they speak with increasing authoritativeness to urban officials and policy makers.

Finally, social science researchers need to throw off the obsolete assumption favored as late as the 1950s and the 1960s and still prevalent in some quarters, that the scientific approach to studying human behavior demands an objective, personally uninvolved investigator. We now know that the initial bias in any research comes with the identification and definition of issues to be studied. Participatory research is the social scientist's way of showing his or her commitment to people's well-being, rather than to institutional structures or political stability. By treating people in poor communities as partners in the research enterprise, rather than as unequal, dependent, or alienated subjects or objects, and by collaborating with people in designing and carrying out inquiries that primarily meet their needs at family and community levels and secondarily address academic or national developmental needs, we will be putting our professional expertise—and our humanity—to the test.

References

Austin, J. E. *Urban Malnutrition: Problem, Assessment, and Intervention Guides.* Summary submitted to the World Bank. Cambridge, Mass.: Harvard University, 1976.

Buvinic, M., Youssef, N. H., and Von Elm, B. *Women-Headed Households: The Ignored Factor in Development Planning.* Report submitted to AID/WID. Washington, D.C.: International Center for Research on Women, 1978.

Cornelius, W. A. *Urbanization and Political Demand Making: Political Participation Among the Migrant Poor in Latin American Cities.* Migrant and Development Study Group. Cambridge, Mass.: MIT Center for International Studies, 1975.

Cousins, W. J., and Goyder, C. *Changing Slum Communities.* New Delhi: Indian Social Institute and Manohar, 1979.

Davis, K. *World Urbanization 1950-1970.* Vol. 2. *Analysis of Trends, Relationships, and Development.* Population Monograph Series, no. 9. Berkeley: University of California, 1972.

Hollnsteiner, M. R., and Lopez, M. E. "Manila, the Face of Poverty." In T. Icinose (Ed.), *Asia Urbanizing: Population Growth and Concentration and the Problems Thereof.* Tokyo: The Simul Press, 1976.

Laquian, A. A. "Issues and Instruments in Metropolitan Planning." Paper presented to United Nations Fund for Population Activities international conference on population and the urban future, Rome, September 1-4, 1980.

Mahadevan, M. "Face to Face with Poverty — the Mobile Crêches, India." In UNICEF, *The Situation of Children in Asia.* Bangkok: Regional Office of UNICEF for East Asia and Pakistan, 1977.

Murphy, D. "Mother India." In D. Murphy (Ed.), *The Bishop's Dog and Other Stories.* Manila, Philippines: Communication Foundation for Asia, 1981.

Paton, A. *Cry, the Beloved Country.* New York: Charles Scribner's Sons, 1948.

Sandell, M., and Sandell, G. "Mortality and Survival Rates of Children of Kanpur Corporation Born in 1969 and Followed Up for Five Years." *Archives of Child Health,* 1981, *22* (2).

Taçon, P. "MY CHILD NOW: An Action Plan on Behalf of Children Without Families." UNICEF document, 1981a, and MY CHILD MINUS TWO, 1981b.

Ungsongtham, P. "Development of Education and Welfare Programmes for Children in Klong Toey Slums, Bangkok, Thailand." *The Situation of Children in Asia, 1977.* Bangkok: UNICEF Regional Office of East Asia and Pakistan, 1977.

United Nations. "Urbanization: Development Policies and Planning." *International Social Development Review,* No. 1. Department of International Economic and Social Affairs, 1968.

United Nations. *Patterns of Urban and Rural Population Growth.* Population Studies no. 68. New York: United Nations Department of International Economic and Social Affairs, 1980.

United Nations International Children's Emergency Fund (UNICEF). *An Analysis of the Situation of Children in India.* New Delhi: UNICEF, 1981.

Mary Racelis Hollnsteiner is senior policy specialist for community participation and family life at the United Nations Children's Fund. She travels extensively in Asia, Africa, and Latin America in support of government efforts at building grass-roots participation into development programs. Prior to joining UNICEF, Dr. Hollnsteiner was professor of sociology and anthropology at the Ateneo de Manila University and was concurrently director of the Institute of Philippine Culture, the university's social science research organization. Her research and publications have focused on issues relating to poverty, urbanization, grass-roots organizations, and roles of women in the Philippines and Southeast Asia.

Peter Taçon is presently UNICEF's regional adviser on children without families for Latin American and the Caribbean. A native of Canada, he worked with the government and in the field of education for fifteen years before shifting his attention to Central and South America. There he addressed the problems of abandoned or street children under the auspices of the Canadian Save the Children Fund, Pueblito Canada, and Pueblito Costa Rica. A child psychologist by academic training, he has developed programs for and written extensively about children without families.

Microlevel analysis and inferential statistics offer some clues to high infant mortality rates in parts of the Third World.

Socioeconomic Determinants of Infant and Child Mortality in Developing Countries

Susan Cochrane
Kalpana Mehra

In 1979, the World Health Organization sponsored a conference on the socioeconomic determinants and consequences of mortality, which marked the beginning of an expanded interest in this topic. For a number of reasons, this interest has been focused on infant and child mortality in developing countries. First, improved techniques now allow us to estimate such mortality independently of vital registration systems. Second, progress in reducing mortality in developing countries seems to be slowing down (Gwatkins, 1979), and this slowdown is believed to derive in large part from the lack of progress in development generally. One major policy question needs to be addressed: To what degree is decline in mortality constrained by socioeconomic development and/or by government policies and programs in developing countries? The answer to this question cannot be simple, however, because socioeconomic development interacts with government policies and programs in numerous ways.

In this chapter we shall review the existing microlevel data on the socioeconomic determinants of mortality and then try to address the question of how these factors relate to government programs and policies. While we know a great deal about the biological causes of mortality, we know very little about the complex social, individual, and behavioral factors that contribute to contracting or recovering from disease or injury. Therefore, at this point we are simply trying to get a rough topology of the relationships and the causal mechanisms that may explain them.

The Evidence: Socioeconomic Differentials

A considerable number of studies have used cross-national or cross-regional associations between mortality and such socioeconomic factors as income and education. While these studies provide some useful insights, there is reason to believe that variables such as income and education are highly correlated with such other factors as access to health care, presence of disease vectors, and so on, that are difficult to measure. Thus, there tend to be systematic errors in estimations of the effects of measured socioeconomic variables on mortality. There also exist other types of statistical aggregation problems that make the use of household and individual data preferable for analyzing the determinants of mortality.

Education is the socioeconomic variable most commonly included in mortality studies; it is much easier than income to measure and has been found to be closely and systematically related to infant and child mortality. Therefore, differentials in infant and child mortality by parental (usually maternal) education give an excellent first approximation of the magnitude of possible effects of socioeconomic factors on infant and child mortality.

In developing countries, data at the household level are becoming increasingly available, as indirect techniques for mortality estimation are applied to census and survey data from developing countries. Tables 1 and 2 summarize the relationships between maternal education and two measures of child mortality.

Table 1 shows the relationship between the proportion of children dying by the age of two years and maternal education for twelve Latin American and three Near Eastern and Far Eastern countries. Table 2 shows the same relationship for ten African countries. Tables 3 and 4 show the proportion of children dying — categorized by mother's age and maternal education — for five Asian and five African countries, respectively. Except for Hong Kong, where mortality is extremely low, the relationship between mortality and mother's education is almost uniformly inverse. It is interesting to note that even a small amount of education (one to three years) is significant in reducing child mortality. The magnitude of difference between levels of education varies substantially, but generally increases with the amount of education received. In many countries, the most educated women have a mortality rate of their children that is less than half the rate of the least educated women. For example, in Kenya (for women between the ages of twenty-five and twenty-nine), it is only about 12 percent and in Guatemala it is 15 percent of mortality for least-educated mothers. These differentials have been examined by Cochrane, O'Hara, and Leslie (1980), and there are systematic patterns in the differentials. For the material in Tables 1 and 3, an additional year of schooling reduces the proportion dying by an average of 9 per 1,000. The materials for Africa included in Tables 2 and 4 were not available at the time of the earlier study, and it is difficult to quantify comparable differentials, since the years of schooling for various educational levels are not readily available. Nevertheless, the data do confirm strong inverse relationships between education and child mortality in Africa, as elsewhere.

While education is the easiest measure of socioeconomic groupings, the educational differentials tell us relatively little about its causal relationships, because education is correlated with income and urban residence, as well as with improved knowledge of and access to medical facilities and with a wide variety of other factors that may affect mortality. Here we see the need for multivariate analysis.

Microlevel Analysis: Multivariate

Considerable work is now being done by demographers and economists on determinants of mortality for individual women and children. Problems addressed and techniques used vary substantially between the two groups of researchers. Demographers have carried over their work on indirect techniques to develop methodologies at the individual level that control very carefully for the child's risk of exposure to mortality. Trussell and Preston (1981) and Boulier and Paqueo (1981) present excellent examples of these concerns. Economists, in contrast, have been more concerned with the policy implications of research. The major methodological issue that economists have examined is that of the endogenous nature of health inputs (O'Hara, 1980).

The issues of controlling for exposure, modeling correctly to avoid confusions arising from endogenous variables, and policy are all important in analyzing the determinants of mortality. We shall deal first with how we can control for the exposure to risk and then with the modeling of the determinants of mortality. The microunit of analysis can be either the individual child or all children of a given woman. In the first instance, the control for exposure is the time elapsed since the child's birth. Since mortality is related to exposure in a nonlinear fashion, exposure control must be nonlinear. The simplest solution is to use a quadratic formulation in a regression equation, with exposure being measured by time since birth; Cochrane (1981) has used this formula. In some instances, this is the best solution that can be found. Whenever possible, however, it is useful to try to separate out period of exposure from time period in which the exposure took place; this procedure is impossible with the preceding approach. Therefore, if the events being examined occurred over a long period of time, some other form of control will be useful.

An alternative formulation is to specify whether a particular child

Table 1. Proportion of Children Dying from Birth to Age Two by Education of the Mother

Country	Year	Total	Number of School Years Attended by the Mother				
			None	1 to 3	4 to 6	7 to 9	10 plus
Bolivia	1971-72	.202	.245	.209	.176	.110	—
Chile	1965-66	.091	.131	.108	.092	.066	.046
Colombia	1968-69	.088	.126	.095	.063	.042	.032
Costa Rica	1968-69	.081	.125	.098	.070	.051	.033
Dominican Republic	1970-71	.123	.172	.130	.106	.081	.054
Ecuador	1969-71	.127	.176	.134	.101	.061	.046
El Salvador	1966-67	.145	.158	.142	.111	.058	.030
Guatemala	1969-70	.149	.169	.125	.085	.058	.026
Honduras	1969-70	.140	.171	.129	.099	.060	.035
Nicaragua	1966-67	.149	.168	.142	.115	.073	.048
Paraguay	1967-68	.075	.104	.080	.061	.045	.027
Peru	1967-68	.169	.207	.136	.102	.077	.070
Thailand[a]	1970	.075	.095	—	.073	—	.023
Jordan[b]	1972	—	.155	—	.092	—	.065
Malaysia[c]	1975	.056	.074	.057	.040	—	.028

[a] Knodel and Chamratrithirong (n.d.)
[b] Majayata, 1975.
[c] Personal correspondence from DaVanzo (n.d.)
Source (for Latin American countries): Arriaga, 1979b, Table 18.

survived to a given age (one to five years), a technique that has been widely used. In this case, a regression model could also include the data of birth, and that data would be used to measure trend factors (Habicht and others, 1981). The major problem with this technique is that it requires accurate reporting of age and of dates when events occurred. Unfortunately, inaccuracies in the reporting of specific ages often occur. Many children dying at ten or eleven months, for instance, are reported as having been one year old at the time of death. Therefore, the ages of two or three are better cutoffs if the reporting of ages or of dates of events is questionable. The most specific control for exposure to risk is that used by Boulier and Paqueo (1981). They used logits of the probability of surviving from birth to the data of the survey as an explanatory variable in their regressions. This technique requires accurate data on date of birth, as well as a specified mortality function. (The functional shape is obtained from life tables, and the levels are selected from the data on mortality of the survey.) One last point about the analysis of the survival of a child: Since this is a zero/one variable, probit is more appropriate than ordinary least squares in the analysis. Authors have differed in how they have dealt with this problem. Behrman and Wolfe (1979) use probit; most others either ignore the problem or else discuss it but do not explicitly use probit. In our Nepal data (Cochrane, 1981), we found that the use of probit did not change the pattern of significance.

Table 2. Proportion of Children Dying by Education of Mother for Some African Countries

	Child's Age (in years)	No School	Education of Mother Elementary	Above Primary		
Ethiopia[a]	0–2	.179	.137	.012		
Gambia[a] (1973)	0–2	.275	.194	.118		

		No School	Primary	Post-Middle		
Ghana[b]	0–1	.1294	.1156	.0821		
	0–2	.1659	.1476	.1016		
	0–5	.2229	.1552	.1132		

		No School	1–4	5–9	Form 1–4	Form 5+
Kenya[a] (1969)	0–2	.160	.122	.090	.053	.033

		Illiterate	Literate			
Sénégal[c] (1973–77)	0–1	.1202	.0714			

		No School	Primary	Post-Primary		
Sierra Leone[a] (1974)	0–2	.292	.217	.140		

		No School	Some Education	Elementary	Higher	
Sudan[a] Rural	0–2	.212	—	.151	—	
(1973) Urban	0–2	.195	.114	—	.077	
Tanzania[d] (1967)	0–5	.261	.192	.132	—	

		No School	1–3	4–7	Secondary	
Uganda[e] (1969)	0–2	.181	.150	.108	.056	
	0–3	.206	.164	.119	.066	
	0–5	.242	.188	.146	.075	

		No School	Lower Primary	Upper Primary +		
Zambia[a]	0–2	.174	.165	.093		

[a] Ramachandaran, 1979.
[b] Tawiah, 1979.
[c] République du Sénégal, 1981.
[d] Egero and Henin, 1973.
[e] Republic of Uganda, 1976.

These types of analyses of the survival of individual children require data on specific births. Birth-history data provide the greatest information, but collection is time-consuming and the quality of data on the timing of births and deaths is questionable. Data on the most recent birth in a family is easier to collect and is probably more accurate with respect to dating. Unfortunately,

Table 3. Proportion of Children Dying by Age and Education of Mother (Selected Asian Countries)

Country	Mother's Age (in years)	No School	Some Primary	Upper or Completed Primary	Beyond Primary	Completed Secondary
Hong Kong	20-24	.000	.000	.000	.000	—
(1971)	24-29	.014	.005	.007	.000	—
	30-34	.004	.009	.003	.016	—
Indonesia	20-24	.174	.171	.090	—	—
(1976)	25-29	.164	.164	.112	—	—
	30-34	.219	.199	.118	—	—
Republic of Korea	20-24	.084	.064	.051	—	.000
(1965-66)	25-29	.110	.087	.058	—	.049
	30-34	.137	.104	.077	—	.054
Pakistan	20-24	.231	.147	—	.136	—
(1975)	25-29	.209	.172	—	.109	—
	30-34	.213	.141	—	.086	—
Philippines	20-24	.103[a]	—	.066	.051	—
(1973)	25-29	.083	—	.067	.043	—
	30-34	.093	—	.088	.045	—

[a] Includes grades 1-4.
Source: Constructed from several tables in Arriaga, 1979a.

there is some skepticism in the literature on whether all births (or the correct births) are recorded (Hill, 1981). The reference-period technique described above is more successful in recording events, as well as more accurate in dating, by its use of the reference event. The technique's only limitation, from an analytical point of view, is that only a fraction of the households included in the survey will have an event in the reference period. Consequently, analysis of the determinants of mortality will have to be confined to a subsample. In addition, this subsample is not random with respect to the determinants of mortality if fertility and mortality are determined by some of the same factors. Those households that have lower birthrates will be underrepresented in the sample. While this does not bias estimates of infant mortality for the whole sample (since that is a period-specific measure), it could distort the differentials. Whether this distortion is serious or not is uncertain, but the loss in overall sample size is important. (A related problem arises if the most recent birth is used. In that case, those with lower fertility will have, on the average, most-recent children who are older; therefore, the exposure occurred when birthrates were generally higher. This pattern of distortion differs, however. More-

Table 4. Proportion of Children Dying by Age and Education of Mother
(Selected African Countries)

Country	Mother's Age (in years)	No School	Primary	Beyond Primary
Botswana	20-24	.144	.109	.056
(1971)[a]	25-29	.176	.123	.068
	30-34	.182	.141	.071

Country	Mother's Age (in years)	Illiterate	Read and and Write	Primary	Preparatory
Cairo, Egypt[b]	20-24	.17	.13	.11	.09
(1976)	25-29	.17	.13	.09	.08
	30-34	.17	.12	.09	.07

Country	Mother's Age (in years)	No School	Some Primary	Upper or Completed Primary	Beyond Primary	Completed Secondary
Kenya[c]	20-24	.169	.127	.088	.048	.047
(1969)	25-29	.192	.132	.094	.061	.024
	30-34	.219	.146	.115	.059	.025
Nigeria	20-24	.108	—	.076	.056	.074
(1977)[d]	25-29	.135	—	.112	.083	.062
	30-34	.183	—	.131	.089	.040

Country	Mother's Age (in years)	No School	Primary	Secondary
Zimbabwe[e]	20-24	.16	.10	.06
(1969)	25-29	.18	.11	.05
	30-34	.20	.13	.06

[a] Republic of Botswana, 1971.
[b] Abou-Gamrah, 1980.
[c] Republic of Kenya, 1971.
[d] Sembajwe, 1977.
[e] Rhodesia, 1971.

educated women in their twenties usually have their children closer together, even though they have fewer children overall.)

Proportion of Children Surviving

Data on the total number of children born to a woman and on the number of children who have died, combined with data on the mother's age or marital duration, are the minimum data required to analyze mortality. As for child-specific analysis, the control for exposure to risk of dying is crucially important. At a minimum, the age of the mother can be used in the regression as an explanatory variable. At the other extreme, child deaths for a specific woman can be standardized for expected deaths on the basis of mortality and fertility schedules. There are, however, important trade-offs in these statistical techniques. Trussell and Preston (1981) have discussed the general trade-offs among maternal age, marital duration, and time since birth of the first child. Marital duration is generally preferred, given the greater specificity and standardization of the work related to it. If first-birth intervals are long, however, or if informal cohabitation is common, then time elapsed since birth of the first child is preferable.

Since interaction can be expected between exposure and the other variables affecting mortality, the use of age, marital duration, or age of the oldest child in the regression equation is the least-preferred solution, but in some cases it is the only one that the data will permit. For large samples, it is possible to use separate regression to analyze mortality for mothers of different age groups. This is the technique that has been used by Rosenzweig and Schultz (1981) for data from the Colombian census, where the smallest size for an age–residence group was 3,068.

The third technique that is used to control for exposure is standardization of deaths by expected deaths, given exposure. To use this technique, however, requires knowledge of birth timing and use of an appropriate mortality model or of an assumed mortality and fertility schedule. If a fertility schedule is assumed, then actual deaths will deviate from expected deaths, because of differences in fertility and mortality assumptions. The kinds of biases introduced into the analysis by such a procedure seem too great to allow standardization by expected deaths, unless the age pattern of fertility is known for each woman.

Another technique that can be used to control for exposure requires data on the age of death and on the current age of each of a woman's children. This technique uses a dependent variable — proportion of children surviving to a given age. Knowles (1979) has used the proportion of children surviving to age three as a dependent variable. While such data are generally obtained from a birth history, an abbreviated method is to ask what the age at death was for each child reported to have died, and the age of the youngest child and of the next youngest and possibly of the third youngest, to be sure (1) of the number of all children born to a woman and (2) that they were born long enough ago to have spent three, five, or x years at risk of death. An alternative is to ask how many children were born in the last x years and how many have survived. Such data would be useful for analyzing the labor supply of men and children as well as of women.

Finally, with respect to analysis of the data on the proportion of children surviving, ordinary least squares are generally inappropriate since the dependent variable is constrained between zero and one. Using regressions on aggregate units, Trussell and Preston (1981) concluded that use of ordinary least squares gives the same pattern of sign and significance as the use of more elaborate and expensive techniques. (Whether this conclusion also applies to the analysis of microdata sets with continuous, rather than categorical, independent variables is not completely clear.) Similarly, Knowles (1979) found the results of using more elaborate techniques did not differ from those based on use of ordinary least squares in terms of sign, significance, or R^2s.

Results of the Analysis

Table 5 summarizes the results of recent microstudies of the determinants of mortality. (There are few older studies on this topic that use microdata, although many have used geographical aggregates for the analysis of mortality with regression techniques; see Cochrane, O'Hara, and Leslie, 1980, for a review of the two types of studies as of early 1980.) The main questions to be addressed in examining these results are: Does the methodology of measurement and control for exposure affect the significance and signs of the results? What are the policy implications of the results? With respect to the first question, the use of different samples complicates matters. Ideally, different analyses should be run on the same data set, as was done by Trussell and Preston (1981) Only accidentally do we have such controlled experiments. See Cochrane (1981), Butz and DaVanzo (1978), Habicht and others (1981), Knowles and Anker (1975), and Anker and Knowles (1982).

The results indicate that the determinants of mortality are not well known. The highest R^2 is 0.14, and this figure appears if survival of previous children is included in analyzing the mortality of the most recent birth (Cochrane, 1981). There does not seem to be a systematically higher explanatory power with one form or another of the dependent variables. In addition, different patterns of significance do not appear to depend on technique.

One important finding is that the sex of the child is important is explaining both mortality and the factors that affect mortality. This gender effect is not entirely biological. In those samples with strong son-preference—rural India and Nepal—female mortality is higher. (It is marginally higher for females, in Cochrane, 1981; it is much larger for females for postneonatal period, in Simmons and Bernstein, 1981). In other cases, males are at a significant disadvantage. While sex of children is not a policy variable, this information may help in the targeting of health programs. If this factor is believed to be important, then child-specific analysis will be necessary.

Survival of the last child can also allow us to sort out the causal relationship between fertility and mortality, which is not possible on the basis of the proportion of children surviving. We can use the number of previous births (parity) or the total number of children born in an equation explaining

Table 5. Summary of Microanalysis of the Determinants of Mortality

A. Unit of Analysis: The Child

Study	Sample Size	Proportion Dying	Control for Exposure	Estimation Technique R^2	Explanatory Variables (sign of significant variables in parentheses) Dependent Variable Converted to Survival	Policy Implications
Anker and Knowles (1982) Kenya	5,597–6,305	.06	Survival to age 3	OLS[1] .02	Year (+); male (+); malaria (−); income (+); maternal education (+); father's ed; pit latrine (+); water source; thatched roof; use of hospital; use of traditional medical care (−); poor maternal health	The policy variables except for education are either endogenous or insignificant. Therefore, it is difficult to derive policy conclusions.
Boulier and Paqueo (1981) Korea and Sri Lanka	2,196–6,357	.032–.087[2]	Logit of life table survival probabilities at each age	Logit (Separate equations for six residence groups)	<table><tr><th></th><th colspan="4">Korea</th><th colspan="4">Sri Lanka</th></tr><tr><th></th><th colspan="2">Male</th><th colspan="2">Female</th><th colspan="2">Male</th><th colspan="2">Female</th></tr><tr><th>Variable</th><th>U</th><th>R</th><th>U</th><th>R</th><th>U</th><th>R</th><th>U</th><th>R</th></tr><tr><td>Mother<19</td><td>0</td><td>0</td><td>0</td><td>0</td><td>−</td><td>0</td><td>−</td><td>0</td></tr><tr><td>Mother>30</td><td>+</td><td>0</td><td>0</td><td>+</td><td>0</td><td>+</td><td>0</td><td>0</td></tr><tr><td>1st birth</td><td>0</td><td>−</td><td>−</td><td>−</td><td>0</td><td>0</td><td>+</td><td>0</td></tr><tr><td>Birth order</td><td>−</td><td>−</td><td>−</td><td>−</td><td>−</td><td>−</td><td>0</td><td>−</td></tr><tr><td>Mother's ed</td><td></td><td></td><td></td><td></td><td></td><td></td><td></td><td></td></tr><tr><td>Some prim.</td><td>+</td><td>+</td><td>0</td><td>0</td><td>0</td><td>0</td><td>0</td><td>0</td></tr><tr><td>Complete prim.</td><td>+</td><td>0</td><td>0</td><td>0</td><td>+</td><td>+</td><td>+</td><td>+</td></tr><tr><td>Tamil</td><td></td><td></td><td></td><td></td><td>0</td><td>−</td><td>−</td><td>−</td></tr></table>	No policy variables except education
Habicht and others, (1981) Malaysia	5,357–5,584	.01–.05	Survival to 5 different ages	OLS (5 specifications) .01–.13	*Proximate variables*: maternal age (+); # of pregnancies in 24 months (−); proportion stillbirths (−); Chinese (+); Indian (+); parity; male (−); birth weight (+) *Direct correlates*: breastfeeding (+); supplements; exclusive toilets (+); community sanitation; water source (only piped is significant) (+); place of delivery; density; use of medicine man (−)	Community water supply and toilets have no effect unless a child is not breastfed

Butz and Da Vanzo (1978) Malaysia	4,067	Survival to age 1	OLS (Several specifications) .07	Length of breastfeeding (+); birth weight (+); male (−); other pregnancies in 15 months (−); maternal ed; sanitation (+); house quality; distance to clinic; infant foods available (+)	Sanitation, hospital and the availability of infant foods significantly increase survival
Cochrane (1981) Nepal (Rural Terai)	490 (last birth only)	Time since birth (quadratic)	OLS (Probit shows no difference) .07–.14	Female (−); cattle ownership; house type; landownership; survival of previous children (+)	Wife's education too rare to be studied. Husband's literacy affects survival indirectly through survival of previous children
Simmons and Bernstein (1981) Rural Uttar Pradesh	1,131–1,306	Neonatal death Post-neonatal	OLS (Separately by sex) .03–.20	*Neonatal (tetanus) death:* time to hospital; village mortality; education; large animals (−); prior tetanus deaths (−); untrained attendant (−); child of that sex wanted (+) *Neonatal (non-tetanus):* same variables included as above; only ones significant are: time to hospital (− for males only); village survival (+ for females only); untrained attendant (− males only); up to God (− males only) *Post-neonatal:* M – village survival (+); female ed (+); family support (mixed); parity (+); females wanted (−) F – no education (−); mother's ed (+); male competitor (−); female children wanted (+); up to God (−)	Policy variables rarely significant
Behrman and Wolfe (1979) Nicaragua	153–1,871	Time since birth	Probit (total and separately by region) .02–.09	Other income; wife's predicted income; wife's schooling (+); wife's age; wife's informal sector work; male present; male ed; household size; births in the last 5 years (−); caloric intake; refrigerator; never migrated; low birth weight (−); pre-natal care; medical attendant; rural; breastfeeding; public sewers (+); density; parasites	Public sewers are significant as is maternal education. Other potential policy variables are endogenous.

[1] Ordinary Least Squares (OLS)
[2] The authors do not report number of proportion dead in six resident groups, but report values of /x for ages 1, 5, and 15 for each group. These values are used to obtain the mortality range given above.

Table 5. Summary of Microanalysis of the Determinants of Mortality (continued)

B. Proportion of Children Surviving

Study	Sample Size	Proportion Dying	Control for Exposure	Estimation Technique R^2	Explanatory Variables (sign of significant variables in parentheses) Dependent Variable Converted to Survival	Policy Implications
Anderson (1979) Guatemala	638	Not given	Proportion surviving relative to expected	OLS Specification H_3 .05	Education of wife; education of husband (+); wealth; towns (sign differs by town)	Education is the only policy variable
Cochrane (1981) Nepal	502	.25	Time since 1st birth	OLS .03–.05	Husband's literacy (+); children ever born (−); cattle ownership; district	Education is the only policy variable
Knowles (1979) Karachi	505	.12	Proportion surviving to age 3	OLS Logit .11	Husband's literacy (+); wife's literacy; income per capita (+); supplement; breastfeeding (+); breastfeeding squared (−); solid food; water; toilet; refuse collection (+); use of private physician (+); use of dai (+)	Policy variables are generally endogenous

Knowles and Anker (1975) Kenya	456	Wife's age[3] at first birth	OLS .09	Wife's education (+); urban resident (+); lowland residence (−); household income; birth spacing; length of breastfeeding	No policy variables except education
Rosenzweig and Schultz (1981) Colombia	3,068–13,304	Proportion of children dying relative to averages for age, residence groups	OLS .003–.05	W/o interactions, temperature and food prices. Among mother's education (+), maternal age, hospital beds, family planning expenditures per capita, clinics per capita, only mother's education is consistently significant. Clinics increase survival in urban areas only; time to capital generally increases mortality With interaction, with education / without temperature or food prices. Maternal education (+) significant in all cases; clinics positive and significant in urban areas for women over 19 and in two rural age groups. Time to capital increase mortality. Family planning expenditures reduce survival in 3 rural and 1 urban groups. Clinics have a negative interaction with female education in urban areas for women over 19 and for rural women 25–29. Other interactions are generally insignificant.	Women's education systematically reduces mortality. Hospitals have no effect. Clinics reduce mortality in the urban areas. In urban areas, clinics have a greater impact for less-educated than more-educated women.

.065   Not given

---

[3] This is not really an adequate control.

survival of the most recently born child. The evidence is mixed here, however: Boulier and Paqueo (1981) found that higher number of births was associated with lower survival in Sri Lanka and in Korea, but Simmons and Bernstein (1981). These studies specify spacing by number of births in the last x months, four to six births, there was lower mortality for males in the postneonatal period. Cochrane (1981) found that parity per se was not significant in explaining survival of the most recently born child (perhaps because of the small sample size).

The spacing of births had significant effects on child survival for Behrman and Wolfe (1979), Butz and DaVanzo (1978), and Habicht and others (1981). These studies specify spacing by number of births in the last x months, whenever x varies. There is some problem of causation here, since perhaps the survival of previous children affects spacing, rather than spacing's affecting the survival of other offspring. This is what Cochrane (1981) found in Nepal, but that data is small, and the accuracy of the spacing data is suspect. (The inappropriate specifications depend on what we wish to learn about mortality determinants. If we want to know about the effect of the time between births, then it is necessary to use that variable in the analysis, rather than the number of births per time interval.)

Overall, there are certain conceptual reasons for preferring child-specific data to woman-specific data for analyzing the determinants of mortality. All children are not equally useful for analysis; only for recent births is it possible to assume that explanatory variables refer to the appropriate time period. For example, current income or current availability of water are factors unlikely to be relevant to survival ten or even five years ago. Therefore, important trade-offs exist for consideration of the appropriate reference period. For accuracy in collection, the reference period should be relatively short, but for analysis, we want it sufficiently long to allow most households to have a birth, and to have enough children who have been exposed through the most severe risk periods for child mortality.

The results in Table 5 contain some interesting policy implications. First, parental education is an extremely important determinant of infant and child mortality, but it is not always significant, partly because of the failure to separate exogenous from endogenous variables (see O'Hara, 1980). For example, if assistance of a doctor at delivery is used as an explanatory variable, then education's observed effect will be reduced, because a major channel through which education affects survival is that of better health care. Second, the use of medical facilities is not universally significant, nor is access, as measured by distance to clinics. This circumstance may derive from problems of modeling, since use of facilities is in fact endogenous, and those who are in greatest need will use them more. In the United States, for example, use is probably positively related to mortality among those over childhood ages. Third, breastfeeding is related to survival—in some cases linearly, in some cases nonlinearly, and in some cases not at all. What is even more interesting is that the archvillain of nutritionists, infant foods, is positively related to survival in Malaysia (Butz and DaVanzo, 1978). Fourth, the Malaysia Family Life Survey found very interesting interactions between breastfeeding and sources of water, which may explain the lack of consistent effects of either. In areas without pure water, breastfeeding is very important to survival. Where pure water is available, breastfeeding is less significant.

Implications

Direct policy variables are not included in most data sets that have been used to analyze determinants of child mortality, and so most researchers who directly address policy issues have to search out data on communities identified in their household data sets. For this reason, not much thought has been given to exactly how policy can affect mortality. For example, health clinics in rural areas make no difference to mortality in rural Colombia (Rosenzweig and Schultz, 1981). This fact probably arises from naive use of data on clinics: Are the clinics staffed? How frequently do they treat patients? Are there charges for users? What are the qualifications of the staff? Are drugs available?

Rosenzweig and Schultz also found that the availability of clinics increases survival rates in urban, but not in rural, areas, and that travel time to the capital generally increases mortality. The failure of the clinic-availability factor to affect mortality in rural areas may reflect such measurement problems as lack of control for the quality of the clinic. Alternatively, clinics may be ineffective because of a lack of cooperating factors. For example, because of ignorance or superstition, people in rural areas may be unwilling to use clinics. This possibility raises the question of interactions between socioeconomic development and social programs. Rosenzweig and Schultz tested for the interaction of education and availability of clinics. They found this interaction to be significant in urban areas, where the two appear to be substitutes. In rural areas, there appeared to be no significant interaction between education and availability of services.

While the multivariate studies of microdata show significance of education, income, and residence in many cases, and of such policy variables as water source and availability of clinics, the evidence is still too fragmentary to give a very clear picture of the relative importance of the various determinants of mortality. In addition, improving understanding of mortality determinants seems essential to modeling the interactions between socioeconomic variables on the one hand, and programs and policies on the other. This seems to be the next step in the research on determinants of infant and child mortality in developing countries.

References

Anderson, K. H. "Determination of Fertility, Child Quality, and Child Survival in Guatamala." *Economic Growth Center Discussion Paper* (Yale University), 1979, 332, entire issue.

Abou-Gamrah, H. "Fertility and Childhood Mortality by Mother's and Father's Education in Cairo, 1976." Paper presented at CU/ISSR seminar on demography in Egypt, Cairo, December 15-18, 1980.

Anker, R., and Knowles, J. C. *Fertility Determinants in Developing Countries: A Case Study of Kenya*. Liege, Belgium: Ordina Editions, 1982.

Arriaga, E. E. *Infant and Child Mortality in Selected Asian Countries*. Washington, D.C.: U.S. Bureau of the Census, 1979a.

Arriaga, E. E. *Infant and Child Mortality in Selected Latin American Countries*. Washington, D.C.: U.S. Bureau of the Census, 1979b.

Behrman, J. R., and Wolfe, B. L. *The Impact of Health and Nutrition on the Number of Surviving Children in a Developing Metropolis*. University of Pennsylvania, unpublished paper, 1979.

Botswana, Republic of. *Report on the Population Census, 1971*. Gaborone: Central Statistical Office, 1971.

Boulier, B., and Paqueo, V. B. *On the Theory and Measurements of the Determinants of Mortality*. Discussion paper no. 31-31. Washington, D.C.: Population and Human Resources Division, World Bank, 1981.

Butz, W. P., and DaVanzo, J. *Contracepting, Breastfeeding and Birth-Spacing in Malaysia: A Model of Decision-Making Subject to Economic and Biological Constraints*. Working draft WN-10146 AID. Santa Monica, Calif.: RAND Corporation, 1978.

Cochrane, S. H. *The Determinants of Fertility and Child Survival in Nepal Terai*. Discussion paper no. 31-34. Washington, D.C.: Population and Human Resources Division, World Bank, 1981.

Cochrane, S. H., O'Hara, D. J., and Leslie, J. *The Effects of Education on Health*. Staff working paper no. 405. Washington, D.C.: World Bank, 1980.

Egero, B., and Henin, R. A. *The Population of Tanzania: An Analysis of the 1967 Census*. Government of Tanzania: BRALUP and the Bureau of Statistics, 1973.

Gwatkins, D. R. *The End of an Era: Recent Evidence Indicates an Unexpected Early Showing of Mortality Declines in Many Developing Countries*. Washington, D.C.: Overseas Development Council, 1979.

Habicht, J. P., Butz, W. P., and DaVanzo, J. "Changes in the Influences of Family and Community Characteristics on the Mortality of Malaysian Children over the First Year of Life." Paper presented at annual meeting of the Population Association of America, Washington, D.C., March 26-28, 1981.

Hill, K. "An Evaluation of Indirect Methods for Estimating Mortality." Paper presented at the IUSSP Seminar on Methodology and Data Collection in Mortality Studies, Dakar, Senegal, July 7-10, 1981.

Kenya, Republic of. "Mortality and Population Growth." In *Report on the 1969 Census*. Nairobi: Central Bureau of Statistics, 1971.

Knodel, J., and Chamratrithirong, A. "Infant and Child Mortality in Thailand: Levels, Trends, and Differentials as Derived Through Indirect Estimation Techniques." Unpublished manuscript, Population Studies Center, University of Michigan, n.d.

Knowles, J. C. *The Determinants of Mortality in a Low-Income Area of Karachi*. Discussion paper no. 35. Pakistan: Applied Economic Research Center, University of Karachi, 1979.

Knowles, J. C., and Anker, R. *Economic Determinants of Demographic Behavior in Kenya.* Population and employment working paper no. 28. Geneva: International Labor Review, 1975.

Majayata, A. R. A. "A Study of Mortality in Jordan with Special Reference to Infant Mortality." Presented at seminar on mortality trends and differentials in some Arab and African countries, Cairo Demographic Center, December 17-23, 1975.

O'Hara, D. J. "Toward a Model of the Effects of Education on Health." In S. H. Cochrane, D. J. O'Hara, and J. Leslie (Eds.), *The Effects of Education on Health.* Washington, D.C.: World Bank, 1980.

Ramachandaran, K. V. "Fertility and Mortality Levels, Patterns and Trends in Some Anglophone African Countries." Presented at expert group meeting on fertility and mortality levels, patterns, and trends in Africa and their policy implications, UNESCO Economic Commission for Africa, Monrovia, Liberia, 1979.

Rhodesia, Republic of. *1969 Population Census, Interim Report.* Vol. 2. *The African Population.* Salisbury: Central Statistical Office, 1971.

Rosenzweig, J. R., and Schultz, T. P. "Child Mortality and Fertility in Colombia: Individual and Community Effects." Paper presented at the International Symposium on Literacy, Education, and Health Development, Ann Arbor, Michigan, March 17-19, 1981.

Sembajwe, I. S. L. "Fertility and Child Mortality Levels and Differentials Among the Yoruba of Western Nigeria." Unpublished doctoral dissertation, Research School of Social Sciences, Australian National University, 1977.

Sénégal, République du. *Enquête Sénégalaise sur la fécondité, 1978.* Vol. 1. Dakar: Minestre de L'Economie et des Finances, 1981.

Simmons, G., and Bernstein, S. "The Educational Status of Parents and Infant and Child Mortality in Rural North India." Paper presented at the International Symposium on Literacy, Education, and Health Development, Ann Arbor, Michigan, March 17-19, 1981.

Tawiah, E. O. "Some Demographic and Social Differentials in Infant and Early Childhood Mortality in Ghana." Presented at expert group meeting on fertility and mortality levels, patterns, and trends in Africa and their policy implications, UNESCO Economic Commission for Africa, Monrovia, Liberia, 1979.

Trussell, T. J., and Preston, S. H. "Estimating the Covariates of Childhood Mortality from Retrospective Reports of Mothers." Paper presented at the IUSSP Seminar on Methodology and Data Collection in Mortality Studies, Dakar, Senegal, July 7-10, 1981.

Uganda, Republic of. *Mortality—African Population. Report on the 1969 Population Census.* Vol. 4. *The Analytical Report.* Kampala: Statistics Division, President's Office, 1976.

Susan H. Cochrane is senior economist in the policy and research unit of the Population, Health, and Nutrition Department of the World Bank. She joined the bank as a Brookings Policy Fellow in 1976. She has published widely in the field of population economics, as well as in development economics.

Kalpana Mehra has been a research assistant in the Policy and Research Unit of the Population, Health, and Nutrition Department of the World Bank since 1978.

Cultural beliefs can affect childbearing and socialization in ways that cannot be accounted for by the traditional economic models for studying development.

Fertility and Child Development: An Anthropological Approach

Robert A. LeVine

As international aid policies become more concerned with human resources, it seems only logical that these policies should be grounded in scientific knowledge from those fields concerned with human behavior and development, of which the interdisciplinary field of child development is one. It is an important one because policies concerning education, population, health, and the family make assumptions about how childcare and child development relate to adult performance and decision making, assumptions that can be either arbitrary or empirically based, according to the availability of the data and the effort to include them in policy analysis and formulation. Nevertheless, the logical connections between international development and child development—so transparently obvious to those of us with strong interests in both fields—do not guarantee such rapprochement, either in science or in policy. One reason is that policy analysis in the international development field draws its concepts of human behavior largely from economics, in which formal utilitarian models of

This chapter reflects the author's current participation in the Project on Human Potential, supported by the Bernard van Leer Foundation, and in the Population Council Project on Women's Schooling and Fertility, both at the Harvard Graduate School of Education. Comparative research on maternal care and infant development was supported by the National Science Foundation and by the Spencer Foundation.

labor markets provide the primary basis for analyzing microsocial phenomena. In economic analysis, the processes of interest to child development research are most often relegated to a black box between aggregate inputs and outputs, or else they are ignored altogether. The growing interest of economists in a broadening range of societies and social problems has not been accompanied by a similar broadening of theoretical and empirical perspectives or by greater inclusion of those types of data that resist quantification or are unavailable for large populations. The recent interest of economists in human development as an essential factor in economic development does not necessarily signal a more receptive attitude toward disciplines involved in human development research; it may mean only that economists believe it is possible to use the tools of economic analysis to analyze a wider spectrum of issues.

Child development research may be equally unprepared for such a new alliance. The International Year of the Child (1979) only served to emphasize the fact that most child development researchers are Western psychologists operating with experimental models on narrow empirical problems of limited interest outside academic contexts. Socially oriented child research is unusual even in our own society (see Bronfenbrenner, 1979), and questions of relevance to the wider world are rarely considered. Investigators are largely unaware of the international development problems to which their research might contribute.

The picture is not entirely bleak, however. There are not only exceptional investigators in both camps, but also other social scientists, primarily anthropologists and sociologists, who see the value of forging these new connections in an international context. The contributors to this volume exemplify this nascent tendency. In this chapter, I shall offer an illustration of how child development research can be made more relevant to policy analysis in the international development field and of how problem formulation in international development should be broadened to include not only psychological and ontogenetic dimensions but also the perspectives of non-Western cultures.

This chapter concerns fertility and schooling in developing countries. About four years ago, I was asked by the Ford Foundation to survey the evidence relating women's education to maternal and family behavior in the Third World (LeVine, 1980b). I found scarce evidence concerning the problem as it has been conceptualized in child development research—that is, in terms of the mother as a psychological environment for her child—and I had to concentrate my review of the topic on data from my own research group in Africa and the Philippines. I discovered that demographers had found strong and consistent inverse correlations of women's education with fertility and child mortality in Third World countries: More years of maternal schooling, regardless of the quality of education, are associated with fewer births and better rates of child survival. Cochrane (1979) and Caldwell (1979) performed regression analyses on the data available from demographic surveys and showed that the relationships were not simply reflections of differences in material well-being. These studies also pointed out the need for research on the intervening processes involved: What do mothers who have had more years of schooling actually do to account for more of their children surviving than children of mothers who have the same incomes and equal proximity to medical facilities, but less schooling? What happens to more-educated women during their formative years, or in their marital relationships, to account for their wanting and bearing fewer children than do less-educated women in the same socioeconomic situation?

These questions involve environmental influences on the attitudes of young women that affect their behavior as wives and mothers in a particular culturally defined kinship system. To account for the observed correlations in demographic data, it is necessary to collect data of a very different order on the social, cultural, and psychological contexts in which reproduction and mortality take place. Research of this sort requires a willingness to consider the concepts and evidence of several disciplines, from reproductive biology to social anthropology. For example, testing Cochrane's (1979, 1983) suggestion that husband–wife communication affects the schooling–fertility connection entails an examination of family dynamics, while a hypothesis that selection, rather than school influence, accounts for the correlations requires investigations of educational selection and classroom interaction. In this chapter, I shall focus (1) on how cultural patterns of childcare and child development are involved in maintaining and changing fertility rates and (2) on the implications of such patterns for future research and policy.

First of all, it is necessary to place the inverse correlations between women's schooling and fertility in a rough historical context, that is, as primarily associated with long-term social trends in which school attendance is increasing and the birthrate has begun to fall. Western Europe after 1880 was in such a situation, and some Asian and Latin American countries are there now (Van de Walle and Knodel, 1980). At present, however, there are also countries with more stable birthrates, like the countries of tropical Africa, where fertility is high (with crude birthrates of 40 to 50 per 1,000), and the countries of Western Europe, where fertility is low (with crude birthrates of 10 to 18 per 1,000). If we accept the premises of demographic transition theory (Caldwell, 1982), the transitional societies of Asia and Latin America are moving from a position somewhat like that of tropical Africa to one resembling that of contemporary Western Europe. In the transitional sectors of India and Mexico, for example, we find fertility variations at the subgroup level and individual differences that approximate the vast cross-national differences of the contemporary world. A conceptualization of reproductive decision making across this great variety of contexts must be the first step toward solving the specific problems posed by the existing evidence.

The conceptualization I offer here is focused on the determination of parental fertility preferences and the role of ideological factors in stabilizing and changing such preferences. It attempts a more detailed and realistic portrait than I have found in the demographic literature of how women view their reproductive and maternal behavior. Economic models tend to treat parental fertility preferences as though these reflected rational calculations of costs and benefits, on the one hand, and arbitrary tastes, rules, norms, or taboos, on the other. The problem of how these rational and irrational elements are integrated with parental thought and practice is resolved in purely theoretical terms, without reference to actual data. I propose a cultural-mediation model, grounded in comparative studies of parental behavior, in which the varying cultural perspectives available to parents in demographically diverse societies provide the crucial subjective contexts for their experience of the "supply of" and the "demand for" children. This model also takes into account the effects on child behavior of the differing cultural conceptions of reproduction and infant care.

The following propositions, illustrated by Figure 1, provide an outline of the conceptual framework through which we are investigating fertility, maternal behavior, and schooling.

1. Four stages of the demographic transition are recognized. At Stage 1, which was characteristic of all human populations until 200 years ago, mortality and fertility rates were both high, although they varied from one population to another according to the incidence of disease, cultural regulation of the age at which women entered reproductive unions, and the interval between births (LeVine and Scrimshaw, 1983), and cultural practices such as infanticide (Scrimshaw, 1983). Few populations in the world today are at Stage 1. Many are at Stage 2, in which mortality has been lowered by modern medicine and public health measures (particularly immunization, the use of antibiotics, and improved water supplies), although it remains (particularly for infants) far higher than mortality in industrialized countries, in which fertility is as high as or higher than it was in Stage 1 (Nag, 1980). Fertility is often somewhat higher, in fact, because the same medical and public health measures that reduce mortality also improve maternal health and permit mothers to bear more children, while Western influences (including education) tend to abbreviate the birth interval through a shorter period of breastfeeding and postpartum sexual abstinence. Thus, women at Stage 2 have more children than at Stage 1. Cochrane (1983) has found that in the poorer developing countries, primary school attainment for women is associated with bearing more children than women do who have no schooling; it is only among women with secondary schooling that fertility levels off. Women who have been to primary school probably benefit from better health care and may have reduced the period of postpartum breastfeeding and sexual abstinence, but without also adopting contraception. In the wealthier developing countries, however, Cochrane found a linear inverse relationship between women's schooling and fertility, such that even women with primary schooling have fewer children than unschooled women do. This finding probably reflects the transition to Stage 3, in which fertility has become destabilized from its high

Figure 1: A Model of Fertility Determination and Maternal Behavior in Demographic Context

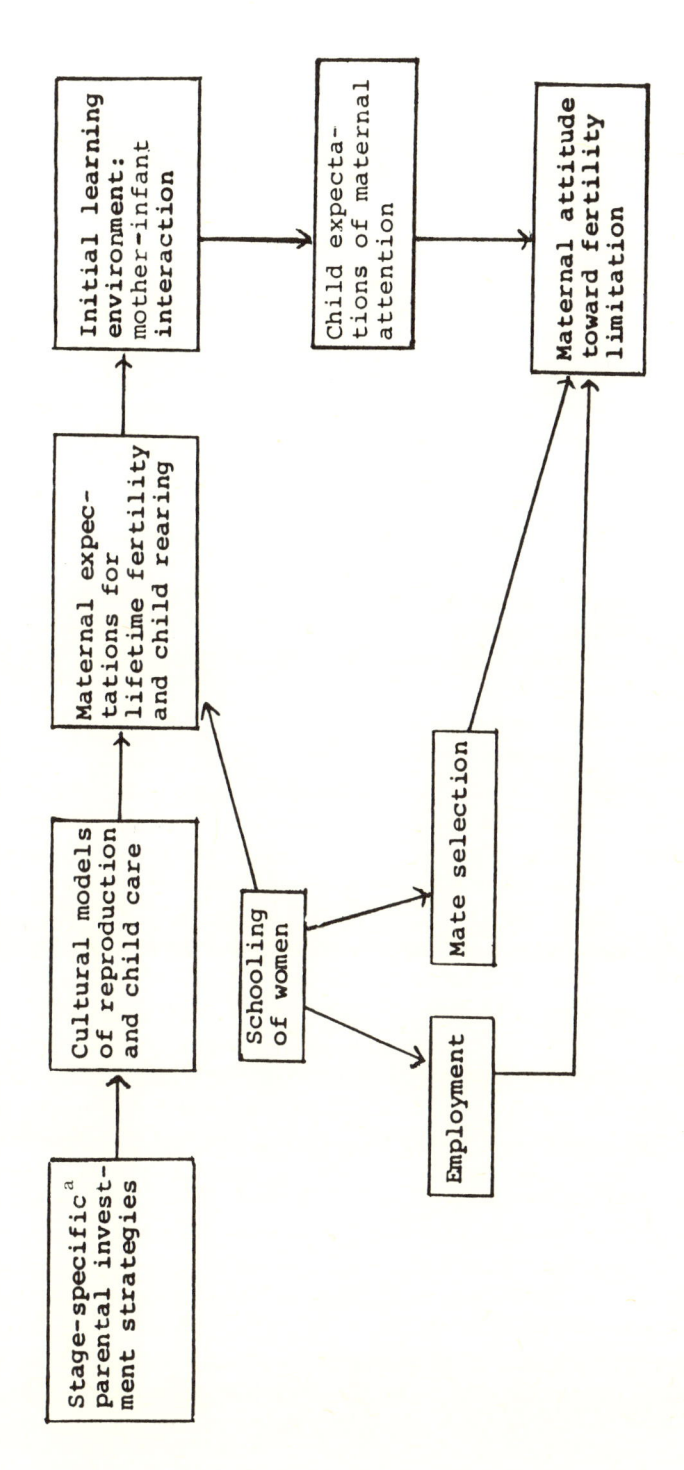

[a] Stages in the demographic transition: Stage 1: Pretransitional (high mortality and fertility); Stage 2: Early transitional (lower mortality, high fertility); Stage 3: Later transitional (moderate mortality, declining fertility); Stage 4: Posttransitional (low mortality and fertility).

level and is beginning to decline. Stage 3 represents populations in which fertility is most variable at the level of individual differences and in which bearing fewer children tends to be associated with such socioeconomic factors as urban residence, female employment, and more education of both spouses. Studies attempting to disentangle the effects of these different factors at Stage 3 have generally shown that a woman's schooling has an independent effect on the number of children she bears, that this effect is stronger than any other single variable, and that it is not attributable simply to its association with other socioeconomic factors or with the postponement of marriage because of prolonged schooling (Cochrane, 1979, 1983). Stage 4 represents populations of stable low fertility, with crude birthrates of 20 per 1,000 or lower, in which mortality is also low. For these populations the transition to low fertility is already accomplished, although there may be substantial differentials in the number of children born, as associated with social classes and regions within each country.

2. Each stage of demographic transition includes a strategy of parental investment that is most adaptive for the socioeconomic conditions typically found at that stage. This strategy is a construct for comparative analysis, representing the optimal pattern of parental care at a given demographic and socioeconomic stage. This representation operates by means of the metaphor of resource distribution, in which *resource* is meant to include parental time and attention, as well as economic goods and other short- and long-term advantages. Parental investment strategies concern how family resources will be distributed among how may offspring, for what period of their lives, toward what conscious goals, and with what actual and imagined returns. It is assumed that the stage-specific strategy constrains cultural variation in the folk models of reproduction and childcare found in populations at that particular stage.

The concept of parental investment strategy can be understood best by illustration. In a Stage 1 society living by family-based agriculture, for example, it makes sense in utilitarian terms to want as many children as possible, because they provide valuable labor during their childhoods—cultivation, herding, carrying water, food processing, infant care—while costing little in space, food, and clothing—items that are often not even subject to calculation in rural settings that have no schools. Furthermore, the more children parents have, the greater the possibilities of filial loyalty and support when parents need it in middle and older age in societies lacking crime protection and old-age pensions.

Nevertheless, parents at Stage 1 often find that their demand for children exceeds the supply. There are no effective remedies for the diseases that cause women to be infertile or to die in childbirth. Parents may lose as many as 20 percent of their infants (those who are born alive) during the first year and another 10 to 20 percent during the next few years. Given this stark reality, parents' primary goal must be child survival, particularly during the first year, when the risk of death is greatest. At the same time, since Stage 1 parents need obedient and low-cost child labor, as well as the long-term loyalty of adult offspring, parents must foster early compliance and avoid encouraging children to expect too much parental attention or other family resources. Whatever resources are diverted to children (for example, maternal attention) are best concentrated on the youngest, whose survival is most uncertain. Thus, the parental investment strategy for Stage 1 societies is assumed to have evolved under the conditions and constraints discussed above. It represents an adaptive response to certain long-term economic and demographic realities, a response likely to retain many of its adaptive values for parents at Stage 2 and even for parents in the rural sectors of Stage 3 populations.

3. Cultural models of reproduction and child development—that is, folk systems of knowledge and conduct concerning those processes—are often formulated in religious, spiritual, and moral terms, but usually make adaptive sense for such practical goals as health and the maintenance of social order in the cultural environments where they evolved. These cultural models thus integrate normative guidance with the pragmatics of family life, and the rationales or explanatory formulas of the models relate rules to environmental contingencies, as well as taking account of the most predictable problems parents face. Although culturally variable, these models are usually experienced as based on common sense, self-evident, and universally valid. Individuals whose reproductive and parental behavior is guided by a cultural model cannot necessarily explain its premises or explicate its most adaptive values, although they usually find that, as in a self-fulfilling prophecy, their own experiences support its logic and confirm its validity.

4. Parental investment strategies in high-fertility agrarian societies favor maximizing child survival, maximizing children's contributions to family economic production during their childhoods, and ensuring their later assistance to aged parents. Parental resources are therefore concentrated on measures designed to increase fertility, reduce infant mortality, and train children in compliance to parental wishes. In low-fertility, urban-industrial societies (Stage 4), parental investment strategies favor limiting fertility as a way of increasing the chances of each child to compete in a labor market. Parental resources at Stage 4 are therefore concentrated on the prolonged development and education of a few children at a cost that is enormous and continually growing, no matter how it is calculated (LeVine, 1980a). At Stage 4, child-rearing is labor-intensive, capital-intensive, and time-intensive for parents, and the qualitative aspects of development replace the number of offspring as a parental goal. There is an analogue here to r-selection and K-selection as strategies of reproduction in animal species (Wilson, 1980, pp. 47–79); but, for humans, variability in the number of offspring and in the amount of parental care is controlled socially rather than genetically.

5. In agrarian societies with high fertility, like the Gusii society of western Kenya, there is a distinctive pattern of maternal behavior and attitude that seems broadly characteristic of rural populations prior to the fertility tran-

sition (LeVine, 1974). In this pattern, maternal attention to the child is concentrated in the first year of life, even during the first few months, depending on the mother's workload. After that, although the mother continues breastfeeding and sleeping with the child at night, maternal attention to a child who is seen to be developing normally tapers off, and the child is increasingly cared for and socialized by older siblings and other children. Caretaking is focused on rapid response to the baby's crying and other distress signals, rather than on encouragement of vocalization or on play. This normally produces a relatively quiet baby, who is easily soothed, undemanding by Western standards, and psychologically prepared both for the displacement that occurs when the mother gives birth again and for early induction into the family work force. This pattern can be seen as an adaptation to what demographers call natural fertility (Knodel, 1983), in which women give birth at regular intervals from marriage to menopause, as well as to the domestic labor needs of agrarian societies.

6. In urban-industrial societies of low fertility, like our own and those of Europe, the period of intensive maternal attention is prolonged. There is less emphasis on soothing and more emphasis on emotionally arousing reciprocal visual and vocal interaction between mother and child. The child is permitted to demand increasing attention from the mother and from other caretakers. This produces more active and less tractable babies and toddlers, who expect increasing rather than decreasing attention to their needs over the preschool years. Since mothers in these societies of controlled fertility tend to bear between one and three children (compared with the Gusii median of ten) and tend to have them all before the age of thirty or shortly thereafter, mothers can accommodate these more demanding children. Furthermore, there is no need for compliant child labor; on the contrary, mother's primary concern is developing children lively and self-confident enough to meet the demands of the competitive school and work systems. These differing goals, situations, and conceptions of child development lead urban-industrial mothers to behave differently toward their infants from the start, as well as generating expectations in infants and small children that are observably different from those of children in agrarian societies (Richman, Howrigan, and New, 1981).

7. In research that we are now initiating on the effects of mothers' schooling on fertility in the Third World, we hypothesize that any ideological influence on an agrarian woman that leads her to lengthen or intensify (in terms of social interaction) the period of early maternal attention will produce a more demanding baby, whose expectancies for increased attention will alter the mother–child relationship toward greater investment of parental resources in each child. This altered relationship, we hypothesize, lies behind the inverse correlations of mothers' education both with infant mortality (Cochrane and Mehra, this volume) and with fertility in developing societies. In other words, we claim that educating women has an influence on their subsequent reproductive and maternal behavior, an influence mediated through their attitudes,

thoughts, and feelings—that is, through deflecting their conceptions of fertility and childcare away from the cultural models of Stages 1 and 2 toward those of Stage 4. At this point, it is possible only to speculate about the educational and psychological processes involved. One line of thinking is that schooling encourages women from agrarian backgrounds to become more assertive in social situations, rewarding them more than their home environments have for active mastery, with the result that women with schooling come to regard themselves as more capable of solving problems and become more inclined to assert their own and their children's interests than women do who have not attended school. Another theory is that schooling, since it enhances reasoning abilities, enables educated women to calculate relationships between ends and means, in family affairs as elsewhere, more effectively than women who have not gone to school. Hence, women with schooling may be better able to understand how health care, hygiene, and nutrition are related to child survival and how birth limitation will help the family economy. There is also the possibility that schooling provides specific information about child health and birth control information that otherwise would not be available. A final possibility is that some combination of these three processes accounts for the correlations of schooling with fertility and with infant mortality in developing countries. Determining which processes of influence actually are operating will make a difference for future policy.

8. We hypothesize that the outcome of extending and intensifying maternal attention to each child varies with demographic stage attained. In populations with high infant and child mortality rates, the outcome is most likely to be enhanced rates of child survival through improved medical care and nutrition. In populations of declining fertility, the outcome is likely to be adopting the goal of limited fertility, given an awareness that each child not only needs but demands more attention. In populations of low fertility, where extended and labor-intensive childcare is taken for granted, differences in maternal ideology about the nature of attention are likely to result in qualitative differences (for example, in the amount of cognitive and social stimulation) in the early childhood environment. For each of these situations, additional maternal schooling is conceptualized as having an ideological influence that results in extending and intensifying childcare and attention. Whether this outcome results from increasing the self-regard, cognitive skill, or information level of each woman, and whether or how schooling has this effect in the diverse social contexts of the contemporary world, is an urgent problem for investigators. The investigation of this problem presents a challenge to research on child development as an interdisciplinary science devoted to producing useful knowledge.

This chapter has shown that the relationship of fertility and infant mortality to women's schooling and maternal behavior is a problem with significant historical, demographic, economic, cultural, and psychological dimensions. (Pediatrics and pedagogy are no less deeply involved, but have been treated here only in passing.) Research on this problem cannot validly ignore these multiple dimensions, yet no investigator nowadays commands an effective knowledge of all the disciplines involved. Perhaps that is why, despite the importance of the problem and the fact that it has been recognized in international development circles for some years, no one has conducted systematic studies of the processes intervening between the schooling of girls and their later attitudes and behavior as mothers. The problem, however, calls for several kinds of experience distinctive to development psychology. First, there is cross-cultural research on mother-infant interaction, represented by the theoretical model proposed here. (See, for example, Field and others, 1981.) Second, there is cross-cultural research on schooling's impact on cognitive development research represented by Wagner's chapter in this volume. Since women in many developing countries have been denied access to education, while their brothers have gone to school, the opportunity to conduct cognitive research on schoolgoing and nonschoolgoing samples exists for females even in countries where most males have long attended school. Third, there is the strong tradition of research design and statistical analysis in developmental psychology. Psychologists working in child development and education have long used systematic methods to disentangle the behavioral effects of co-occurring independent variables. No methodological problem in the schooling-fertility area is unfamiliar to developmental psychologists, who work in natural social settings. Child development specialists can make a unique contribution by shedding new light on this relatively old but increasingly well-documented and greatly important demographic question.

References

Bronfenbrenner, U. *The Ecology of Human Development.* Cambridge, Mass.: Harvard University Press, 1979.
Caldwell, J. C. "Education as a Factor in Mortality Decline: An Examination of Nigerian Data." *Population Studies,* 1979, *33* (3), 395–413.
Caldwell, J. C. *Theory of Fertility Decline.* New York: Academic Press, 1982.
Cochrane, S. H. *Fertility and Education: What Do We Really Know?* Baltimore: Johns Hopkins University Press, 1979.
Cochrane, S. H. "Effects of Education and Urbanization on Fertility." In R. Lee (Ed.), *Determinants of Fertility in Developing Countries.* New York: Academic Press, 1983.
Field, T. M., Sostek, A. M., Vietze, P., and Leiderman, P. H. (Eds.). *Culture and Early Interactions.* Hillsdale, N.J.: Erlbaum, 1981.
Knodel, J. "Natural Fertility: Age Patterns, Levels and Trends." In R. Lee (Ed.), *Determinants of Fertility in Developing Countries.* New York: Academic Press, 1983.
LeVine, R. "Parental Goals: A Cross-Cultural View." *Teachers College Record,* 1974, *76,* 226–239.
LeVine, R. "A Cross-Cultural Perspective on Parenting." In M. Fantini and R. Cardenas (Eds.), *Parenting in a Multicultural Society.* New York: Longman, 1980a.
LeVine, R. "Influences of Women's Schooling on Maternal Behavior in the Third World." *Comparative Education Review,* 1980b, *24,* (2), 78–105.
LeVine, R., and Scrimshaw, S. "The Effects of Culture on Fertility." In R. Lee (Ed.), *Determinants of Fertility in Developing Countries.* New York: Academic Press, 1983.

Nag, M. "How Modernization Can Also Increase Fertility." *Current Anthropology,* 1980, *21,* 27-36.

Richman, A., Howrigan, G., and New, R. "Cultural Styles of Infant-Caretaker Interaction Among the Gusii, Yucatec Mayans, and Bostonians." Paper presented at the Society for Research on Child Development, Boston, 1981.

Scrimshaw, S. "Infanticide as Deliberate Fertility Regulation." In R. Lee (Ed.), *Determinants of Fertility in Developing Countries.* New York: Academic Press, 1983.

Van de Walle, E., and Knodel, J. "Europe's Fertility Transition: New Evidence and Lessons for Today's Developing World." *Population Bulletin,* 1980, *34,* 3-43.

Wilson, E. O. *Sociobiology.* (Abridged ed.) Cambridge, Mass.: Harvard University Press, 1980.

Robert A. LeVine is Roy E. Larsen Professor of Human Development in the Graduate School of Education at Harvard University. He has published widely in the area of comparative child development and personality. His current research is on women and fertility in Mexico.

This chapter provides new evidence that, contrary to previous beliefs, a Third World mother's work outside the home may increase the probability of her children's survival.

The Effect of Maternal Employment on Children's Welfare in Rural Guatemala

Patricia L. Engle

In most parts of the world, women traditionally work in the home, as well as contributing to the well-being of their families through agriculture, manufacturing, and trading. With modernization and urbanization, more and more women are performing paid labor (Boserup, 1970). Because of their lack of training and opportunities, women often must work long hours at low-paying work. Additional training or expansion of job opportunities would increase their productivity, but governmental agencies, convinced that a mother's increased involvement with nonhousehold production would be harmful to her children, resist training and employment programs for women (ICRW, 1980). Current research in the United States indicates that children of women working for wages have as good—or, in impoverished circumstances, better— cognitive, emotional, and nutritional development as children of nonwage-working mothers (Cherry and Eaton, 1977). Little research has been done on

Research for this chapter was supported by a grant from California Polytechnic State University, San Luis Obispo, California. The author would like to express her appreciation for the careful comments and editing of Dan Wagner and Randi Levin on an earlier draft. Responsibility for the finished chapter remains with the author.

this issue in the Third World, and the literature that does exist is conflicting. Because mothers worldwide appear to be increasing their work for earnings, research is urgently needed on how their mothers' working affects Third World children.

This chapter will outline reasons for concern about the effects of maternal employment in the developing world by describing nine mechanisms through which maternal work for income might affect children and by testing the hypothesis that a rural mother's work for earnings can have a positive effect on child survival, the most basic dimension of child well-being.

Previous Research

Definition of Maternal Employment. Women in rural villages have a heavy workload. Fagley (1976) found that in parts of East Africa women work an average of sixteen hours per day. Certain tasks are usually the domain of women: food preparation, childcare, household maintenance, biological reproduction, wood and water collection (the "breeder-feeder" role). Other kinds of work, variously called productive work, market work, or work for earnings, may be performed by some or all women in addition to their household work. For instance, in Guatemala a woman may have a plot of land on which she raises cash crops to sell to neighbors or in a market. Another may run a little store in the front of her house. A third may regularly make more tortillas than her family can use and sell them to neighbors. Yet another will take the bus to the nearby larger town or even to the capital city to work as a domestic servant. In one village, a handicrafts industry for weaving hats from local reeds has developed. All these activities may be called work for earnings or maternal employment.

Three recent changes in maternal employment patterns have led to increased concern about its effects on children. The first change is that, just as policy makers are beginning to realize its extent, modernization of agriculture is eliminating women's agricultural work (Boserup, 1970; Benería and Sen, 1981). Census surveys have often underrated women's work because of the kinds of questions asked and assumptions made. As a result, agricultural extension agents often direct all their efforts toward male farmers, even though women in the Third World produce about half of the food (Fagley, 1975; Blumberg, 1981). The reduction of women's role in food production, as male-oriented technology in agriculture replaces women's small farming plots, is apparently having profound negative consequences for the health and nutritional status of children (Blumberg, 1981). The second change is that, since women's traditional productive roles are being replaced, women are increasingly turning to income-generating activities to provide for themselves and their children (Chaudhury, 1976, in Bangladesh; Tripp, 1981, in Ghana). The third change involves men, who are forced to migrate as seasonal laborers, leaving more women behind to become de facto heads of households (Blumberg, 1981).

How Does Maternal Work for Wages Affect Children?

Effects on children of maternal work for wages may vary importantly with actual working conditions. For example, the mother who works outside the home for twelve hours a day and leaves her year-old baby in the care of her five-year-old may find her infant showing signs of malnutrition and neglect. If the mother works in a shop at the front of her house, where she can watch over her infant, continue to breastfeed her, and earn additional income to purchase supplemental food, then the net effect on the child's nutritional status will most likely be positive. In assessing positive or negative effects on children of maternal work for wages, a major task is to determine which specific factors influence the relationship between employment and children's well-being.

Economists have conceptualized the impact on children of maternal work as the net effect of (1) reduction in the mother's time with children and (2) an increase in her ability to supply them with food, health care, and other purchased goods (Evanson, 1978; Clark, 1979). While this model is useful, it does not consider other important variables, such as availability of childcare, that also probably affect children. From this economic model and additions, two general kinds of variables may be identified: (1) variables concerning direct effects of the ways time and money are used as a consequence of income-earning activities, and (2) variables associated with conditions predisposing women to work. Each type of variable will be discussed below.

Variables Concerning Direct Effects

Increased Income to the Mother. The first and most commonly mentioned benefit of maternal employment is increased income to purchase food and services. Some investigators have suggested that this income will be particularly beneficial for child welfare because it is under the woman's control (Blumberg, 1981). Kumar (1977) found that, among landless peasants in India, income of the mother was more directly related to the nutritional status of the children than was income of the father. One explanation is that income to the male head of household may never reach the family, going instead to other expenditures, such as rent or disposable income (for example, alcohol consumption), as Stravrakis and Marshall (1978) observed in Belize. The effect of having the income within the mother's control has been discussed (Safilios-Rothschild, 1980), but few systematic data are available.

Increase in Maternal Status. A second possible beneficial effect of maternal work is an increase in a woman's status within her family. Some researchers believe that broadening roles of women and improving their status will reduce fertility (Germain, 1975; Reining and others, 1977; see also LeVine, this volume), and that lower fertility will improve conditions for the existing children. This appears to be true for women employed in the formal sector (Abbott, 1974), but women's status may remain low if they are employed in the informal sector, and fertility may not be affected. Maccan and Bamberger (1974) found that much of the work women in Venezuela were able to obtain did not increase their status within the family because it was too poorly paid. In predicting how work affects fertility, Cochrane (1979) concludes, "It is not simply labor participation that must be considered, but the compatibility of work with marriage and childbearing and the wages in that work" (p. 150; see also Cochrane and Mehra, this volume).

Increased Competence and Confidence. Working women have more self-confidence, because they are involved in productive work and in control of some financial resources. Increased confidence and competence can affect children directly if the mother offers a stimulating cognitive and social environment. Children (especially girls) of a working mother may have higher levels of aspiration for schooling in the United States (Hoffman, 1979). In Guatemala, Engle (Engle, Yarbrough, Townsend, and Klein, in press) found that girls' mental test scores increased during a longitudinal study. She suggested that the rural village girls may have observed academic-type activities engaged in by the high-status city women employed by the research project. These potential role models may have influenced the girls' aspirations for schooling and encouraged them to perform better on a mental test battery. The effects of such role models on girls' mental development is a fruitful area for further research.

Reduction in Availability of Maternal Time for Children. Maternal work may have negative effects on children by reducing their time with the mother. This lack of time may limit food preparation, childcare, the feeding of a weaning child, and breastfeeding. Time-use patterns tend to change when women use part of each day in market work. Although the particular pattern or reallocation of time varies according to the situation and the society, some consistencies emerge. Both Popkin (1978) in the Philippines and McGuire (1979) in Guatemala have reported that women who worked outside the home did not substantially reduce their childcare time. Other areas of time use, such as leisure and sleep, are curtailed first. Women tended to work more when an older sibling was available for childcare; evidently, working becomes more possible when an alternative caretaker is available. Only under certain conditions, such as periods of peak agricultural activity (McGuire, 1979) or formal labor force participation requiring ten to twelve hours per day (Rivera, 1979) was mothers' time in childcare considerably reduced.

Nevertheless, studies have shown that, in rural settings, the nonworking mother's time investment in the child drops considerably between the ages of one and two, and the major childcare role is turned over to a sibling or to other relatives in the home (Ho, 1979, and Cabañero, 1978, in the Philippines; DaVanzo and Lee, 1978, in Malaysia; Cain, Khanam, and Nahar, 1979, in Bangladesh; Chavez and Loucky, 1981, in Guatemala).

Breastfeeding. It is often suggested that working mothers will be unable to breastfeed adequately and that maternal employment is one of the primary factors accounting for the decline in breastfeeding, but several studies have found that employment, or working for income, did not result in cessation of breastfeeding in more rural and traditional areas, according to mothers' reports (Greiner, 1979). In some cases, mothers who were unable to breastfeed during the day supplemented during the day and breastfed at night. Social pressures and attitudinal changes have been found to be important predictors of decline in breastfeeding (Greiner, 1979). Haggerty's (1981) results from a sample of 530 periurban Haitian women were similar: A decline in breastfeeding was not linked to maternal employment, but to changes in the social meaning of breastfeeding, but in some less traditional societies, maternal employment may still play a role in the reduction of breastfeeding. Retrospective data from a national sample of Malaysian women revealed marked declines in breastfeeding (DaVanzo and Butz, 1981) over the past thirty years. With education level and other potentially confounding variables controlled, Malaysian mothers who earned very low wages were more likely to breastfeed, whereas those with higher earnings were less likely to breastfeed. The net effect of increased income and decreased breastfeeding on infants' welfare may be either positive or negative, depending on the cost of substitute food, alternative caretakers, and mothers' income.

Quality of Alternative Caretakers. The effect of maternal employment out of the house on children also depends on the quality of the alternative caretakers available. If the caretaker is inferior to the mother, the child may be less adequately nourished and less cognitively stimulated. The most common caretaker that mothers report using is an older female sibling (Engle, 1980), who may be as young as four or five. Little is known about the effects of various kinds of sibling caretakers on the younger child's total development. Weisner and Gallimore (1977) identified a number of important variables, but few studies to date have examined the social or cognitive competence of the child as a function of the type of caretaker available. Thus, alternative childcare systems need additional study.

Variables Associated with Prior Conditions

Women who generate income may be different from those who do not. These differences may have their own independent effects on child welfare and need to be understood separately if the effects of the maternal employment itself are to be determined.

Mother's Education, Health, and Age. Mothers' education is associated with employment, as well as with many child welfare variables. For instance, work in the formal sector is often positively associated with schooling (Engle, 1982), although Behrman and Wolfe (1979) found informal-sector work to be negatively related to schooling. Since working mothers may also be slightly healthier and have better nutritional status (Behrman and Wolfe, 1979), child welfare may also be enhanced. Working mothers are sometimes older than women not engaged in market work (Bloch, 1978, in Senegal; Alfonja, 1981, in Nigeria; and Cabañero, 1978, in the Philippines). Thus, they may have more resources available for their children and fewer infants to take care of.

Marital Status. Because most mothers in the developing world seem to work from economic necessity (see, for example, Rivera, 1979), they are often in the lowest income groups and are also likely to be single heads of households. In Guatemala, single female heads of households are far more likely to be working than are married women, and these single women tend to be among the poorest (Engle, 1982).

Family Economic Level. Since it is well established that poverty, health, and malnutrition are related (Riccuiti, 1977), the effects of maternal employment on children's survival are often confounded with the effects of family wealth. In a review of studies relating maternal work for earnings to infant nutrition in Latin America, Clark (1979) concluded that none of the studies could unequivocally separate the effects of maternal wage work from total family economic status. The clear separation of the influence of maternal employment from prior influence of family economic status is a serious problem for researchers in this domain.

Previous Studies on Maternal Employment

A number of previous studies have specifically considered the effects of maternal income generation on some measure of child welfare. Both positive and negative effects of maternal employment have been found. Tripp (1981) found that maternal occupation in Northern Ghana was more related to children's nutritional status than paternal occupation was. Tripp attributed this finding to the relatively high wage per hour of the women traders and to the value of their income's accessibility to nutritional needs. He reasoned that "the relatively small amount of money that a female trader earns is translated more directly to the nutrition of her children" (p. 20) than is income earned by the father from trading. No other variables were controlled for. Wray and Aguirre (1969) and Haggerty (1981) reported that the type of a mother's work determined whether a positive or a negative association with nutritional status was found. Children of women engaged in part-time or informal-sector work had lowered nutritional levels, whereas the reverse was seen for children of women in higher-paying work. Bloch (1978, in Senegal) found a positive effect of maternal work on girls' play style, which was more goal-directed when their mothers were working than when they were not working.

Negative effects of maternal work have also been reported by some investigators (Levinson, 1974, in India; Battad, 1978, in the Philippines). Behrman and Wolfe (1979) found lower rates of infant survival among urban women working in the informal sector in Managua, but not among those in the formal work sector. Children's health and nutritional status suffered in periods of peak agricultural activity, when the mother spent hours in the fields (Taylor and others, 1971, in India). Popkin and Solon (1976) reported that working mothers were less likely to breastfeed their children but Greiner (1979) in re-examining the data, found that working mothers were more likely to use mixed feedings than exclusive breastfeeding.

These conflicting research findings underline the need for studies that will measure at least some of the intervening variables previously described, as well as conditions of maternal employment and child welfare variables. The large-scale, longitudinal research program described below has provided some key information for resolving these issues.

The INCAP Study in Guatemala

The research presented here on rural Guatemala attempts to test the hypothesis that maternal work for wages has a positive impact on child survival, while controlling for family income, marital status, and maternal education. Specifically, the relationship between maternal employment and child survival and other variables was explored in four rural villages in eastern Guatemala by using multiple-regression techniques. The analysis focused on child survival as a basic indicator of family investment strategies and is related both to health and to nutritional status.

Research for the present chapter was conducted in conjunction with a longitudinal nutritional intervention under the direction of the Institute of Nutrition of Central America and Panama (INCAP). In 1969, four villages from an eastern, Spanish-speaking section of Guatemala, where moderate protein–calorie malnutrition is endemic, were matched on a number of demographic, social, and economic characteristics. The intervention involved differential supplemental feeding of children in four rural villages. From 1969 until March 1977, data on health, home environment, food consumption, and cognitive development were collected on about 1,800 children. A study of fertility behavior, using the same families and conducted in the four villages in 1975, provided the data.

Villages. The families who participated in the study reside in four Spanish-speaking Ladino communities. Nearly all families (83 percent) are engaged primarily in subsistence agriculture. The main crops are corn and beans. Cash crops in this arid region are limited to tomatoes, cassava, and tobacco. There is little permanent migration to or from the communities, although some men and families travel to the coastal zone once a year to harvest cash crops, or else they go to work in other communities as short-term laborers.

The pervasive poverty of these communities is conveyed by the median family income; in 1975, it was approximately $500 per year, of which less than half was available in cash. Families generally live in two-room houses constructed of local materials, mainly adobe. One room serves as a kitchen and the other as sleeping quarters for the whole family, and there is virtually a complete lack of sanitary facilities. Clothing is simple: Women wear simple dresses, and the wealthier ones wear shoes and may own a sweater. The median number of living children per family is four, with a maximum of fifteen. Many children die; 46 percent of the mothers reported having had at least one child die; of these children, 85 percent lived less than a week, whereas only 2.4 percent died after age three. Ethnographies of the villages can be found in Nerlove, Roberts, Klein, Yarbrough, and Habicht (1974) and Mejía Piveral (1972).

Sample and Method. The sample was drawn randomly from all women who were ever married, who were between the ages of fourteen and forty-nine, and who were living in the four villages. A total of 462 women was interviewed. The survey data were drawn from retrospective life histories. Each respondent was asked to recall each childbirth and relate it to other events (such as maternal employment) that occurred during the interval preceding the birth. The interviewers, four Guatemalan women, were trained to reliability on the surveys. Interviewing took place over a six-month period. Each woman was interviewed individually in her home, at her convenience.

Redefining Women's Work. Census figures in developing countries tend to report very low levels of wage earning among women, particularly among poor rural women, partly because a large proportion of their work is in the informal sector. In addition, women themselves do not define much of their work as wage-earning labor. The effect of a specific question asked about work can be seen in the difference among women's responses to three surveys in the four rural Guatemalan villages. Each survey asked women a differently phrased question, so that responses could be compared as a function of which specific question was asked (see Table 1).

The first column of Table 1 contains answers to the question "Did you do anything last year to help yourself financially?" Almost 60 percent of the women answered in the affirmative. (The answers ranged from 25 percent in one village to 82 percent in another.) The second column shows women's responses to the question "Do you work?" Only 45 percent answered *yes* to this question. Women were less likely than in the previous instance to answer *yes* and did not mention agricultural work on their own land and in manufacturing (home crafts) as work roles. In the third column (Sample C) are responses to the question "Do you hold a regular position?" Examples were given to broaden the definition during the interview, but here only 10 percent of the women answered in the affirmative. Women continued to report the occupa-

Table 1. Work Reported by Rural Guatemalan Women as a Function of Three Different Types of Questions

Sample[a]	A: Women with a Child Less than Seven Years Old		B: Women with a Child Less than Seven Years Old (including Ever-Married Women, 14–49)		C: Sample of Ever-Married Women, 14–49, with at Least One Child	
Question	Do things to help yourself financially?		Do you work?		Do you have a regular position?	
Occupation	N	%[b]	N	%	N	%
Agricultural labor in community	15	3.92	4	.69	7	1.50
Agricultural labor out of community	15	3.92	30	5.10	1	.21
Farmer on family land	46	1.20	10	1.73	0	0
Farmer on own land	12	3.13	12	2.07	0	0
Day laborer outside community	0	0	2	.34	0	0
Domestic	18	4.69	20	3.46	15	3.22
Manufacturing, home crafts	54	14.09	96	16.60	13	2.79
Merchant for family agriculture	6	1.56	7	1.21	0	0
Sells what she produces	5	1.30	0	0	0	0
Stationary merchant in community	22	5.74	21	3.63	6	1.29
Transitory merchant in community	13	3.39	36	6.22	4	.86
Specialized labor	17	4.43	24	4.15	2	.43
Blue collar	1	.26	1	.17	0	0
Responding "yes"	224	59.5	263	45.5	48	10.3
Responding "no"	159	41.5	315	54.5	418	89.7
Sample Total	383	100.0	578	100.00	466	100.0

[a] All three samples are from all four villages; they are overlapping but not identical. Each question was asked in a different questionnaire.
[b] Percentages of sample saying "yes"

tions of domestic work, home crafts, and running a store, but they did not mention working on the family farm or selling farm produce as "regular positions." The kind of work reported in response to the third question is probably the most formal and implies longer duration. It will be used in our analyses as the measure of work, simply because it probably plays the largest role in the family's life and generates the most income. Thus, the effects of this work on child survival will be more apparent from Sample C than from the other two samples. Since a relatively small proportion of women reported regular working, the question posed to Sample C can be recoded into a dichotomous variable for the purpose of statistical analyses.

Statistical Analyses of Data from Sample C. The effects of maternal employment on child survival were analyzed using multiple-regression in order to control for the likely confounding variables described previously — maternal education, marital status, and economic level of the family. Maternal education and marital status at the time of the assessment were derived from the mothers' reports. House quality — the number of rooms and quality of floor and walls — was used as a proxy for family economic level. This measure has often been considered as an economic indicator in analyses of the INCAP data (for example, Balderston, Wilson, Freire, and Simonen, 1981). Because the availability of alternative caretakers could reduce the possible negative effects on child survival of maternal work, we attempted to include an indication of the number of adults in the home, measured here by whether the family was nuclear or extended. This variable was also included in the regression model.

The dependent variable was the percent of children born at full term who lived past one year, a direct measure of child survival. As Cochrane (1979) recommends, maternal age at the most recent pregnancy was also included in the regression to control for children's risk of exposure to dying and for other time-associated variables that might affect mortality rates. In addition, analyses were performed using the number of deceased children as the dependent measure, controlling for maternal age. Although the number of deceased children was correlated with child mortality ($r = .49$), the two measures are not identical, and the latter may be a more sensitive indicator of risk factors at the household level. The data were analyzed using an ordinary test squares regression, which, according to Cochrane (this volume), "gives the same pattern of sign and significance as the use of more elaborate and expensive techniques," even when some of the independent variables are categorical.

Description of Variables. Means and standard deviations for each variable used in the multiple-regression analysis are shown in Table 2. The typical mother is not working, has had only one year or less of schooling, and is currently in a union. She lives in a nuclear family in a house with a dirt floor, adobe walls, and one or two rooms. The highest number of living children in the sample is thirteen; the highest number of deceased children is twelve.

Characteristics of Mothers as a Function of Work Status. As has often

Table 2. Means and Standard Deviations of Variables
in Model Based on Sample C (N = 462)

Variable	Mean	Standard Deviation
Work status (0 = no, 1 = yes)	.10	.30
Mother's years of school	1.23	1.48
Age of mother at birth of most recent child	28.70	7.67
Currently married or in a union (1 = no, 2 = yes)	1.92	.27
Family type (1 = nuclear, 2 = extended)	1.27	.44
Floor (1 = dirt, 2 = other)	1.10	.31
Walls (1 = cane, 2 = adobe, 3 = wood or brick)	2.83	1.38
Number of rooms in house (1–4)	1.81	.77
Number of living children	4.09	2.50
Number of deceased children	1.11	1.57
Percent of live children to total births	.81	.22

been reported in the literature, the mothers in this sample who were working were less likely to be in a union (whether married or not) than nonemployed women were (x^2 = 5.82, df = 1, p < .01). There is some evidence that, for these women, work has been necessary to cope with temporary financial instability. Working women currently in a union were much more likely to be with a second or even a third man than were the nonworking women (x^2 = 17.7, df = 1, p < .01). They were also more likely to be living in an extended family than were the nonwage-earning women (x^2 = 3.56, df = 1, p < .05).

A second variable that has frequently been found to differentiate between women with and without stated occupations is years of schooling. Despite the extremely low levels of schooling in this sample, as well as the relative uselessness of formal education for the work that the women were performing, there was a slight association between education and work status (see Table 3). That years of schooling are related to work status in this population is illustrated by the association of years of schooling and work status prior to a woman's first child (t = 3.15, df = 463, p < .01). Maternal age was unrelated to work status.

Contrary to expectations, no relationship between maternal work status and house quality was found. Number of live, dead, miscarried, and aborted children did not differ by work status, but women currently working for income had significantly fewer stillborn births than nonworking women did (see Table 3).

Regression Analysis. Results of the regression analyses are shown in Table 4. Women with a higher proportion of surviving children were younger, better educated, and living in nuclear families. There was surprisingly little relationship between survival rate and house-quality measures (socioeconomic status). A positive relation between maternal work outside the home and child survival was found, but it did not reach significance (p = .20).

The analysis predicting the number of deceased children was consistent

Table 3. T-Tests of Work Status by Child Survival, Maternal Age, and Maternal Schooling[a]

Variable		Number of Cases	Mean	Standard Deviation	T Value	Significance
Number of living children	Nonworkers	418	4.10	2.53	1.04	.29
	Workers	48	3.70	2.25		
Number of deceased children	Nonworkers	418	1.13	1.59	1.36	.17
	Workers	48	.81	1.29		
Percent of living children	Nonworkers	418	.76	.19	−.43	.67
	Workers	48	.81	.22		
Number of abortions	Nonworkers	418	.41	.98	.95	.34
	Workers	48	.31	.65		
Age of mother at interview	Nonworkers	418	31.90	8.79	.39	.70
	Workers	48	31.39	8.32		
Mother's years of schooling	Nonworkers	418	1.20	1.49	−1.50	.13
	Workers	48	1.54	1.40		
Number of stillbirths	Nonworkers	418	.14	.44	1.90	.06
	Workers	48	.06	.24		

[a] Based on a survey of Sample C ($N = 466$)

Table 4. Multiple Regressions for Child Survival and Number of Child Deaths, Controlling for Maternal Education, Family Economic Level and Marital Status[a]

Variable	Survival Rate (Percent of Children Who Survived) b	Survival Rate (Percent of Children Who Survived) F	Number of Deceased Children b	Number of Deceased Children F
Maternal age at most recent birth	−.073	26.46**	.110	82.20**
Maternal education	.019	7.34**	−.078	3.16
House quality				
Floors	.033	.91	.064	.09
Walls	.008	.22	−.064	1.75
Number of rooms	−.014	.93	b	b
Marital or union status (1 = no, 2 = yes)	.059	2.25	.255	1.05
Family type (1 = nuclear, 2 = extended)	−.049	3.71*	.537	11.29**
Work status of mother (0 = none, 1 = some)	.043	1.60	−.346	2.69†
Number of living children	c	c	−.004	.02
R^2	.09		.27	

[a] Based on survey of Sample C ($N = 462$)
[b] Insufficient F-level to enter regression
[c] Not appropriate to analysis
** $p < .01$
* $p < .05$
† $p < .10$

with the results for proportion of surviving children. Mothers with higher numbers of deceased children were older, less well educated, living in extended families, and less likely to be working outside the home. Again, a modest positive relationship between maternal occupation and child survival was found, with controls for the effect of education, economic level, and marital status.

Interpretation of the Regressions. What possible mechanisms could account for the relationship between maternal work and fewer deceased children? Initially, we proposed that two kinds of variables had to be considered — (1) direct effects, or changes in life patterns that result from the mother's time investment in her economic function and from her increased, personally administered income, and (2) associated effects of maternal work, including variables predisposing a woman to become a worker. These variables themselves could influence child survival; examples are overall economic level of the family, the mother's education, and her marital status. The direct effects included a possible negative effect from a lack of the mother's time spent with her children, which would mean inability to prepare time-consuming foods or to breastfeed. There could also be a positive effect, attributed to increased income directly available from the mother.

The surrogate alternative childcare measure—extended (living with husband or wife's parents) or nuclear family residence—seemed to function in the opposite direction from the predictions: Children were consistently more likely to survive in nuclear families than in extended ones. In these villages 73 percent of families are nuclear; it appears to be to stable pattern for older, better-established families ($r = .36$, $df = 460$, $p < .01$ between maternal age and family type). Thus, since much of the childcare in these villages is performed by older siblings, a well-established nuclear family may have as many or more caretakers as a couple or as a single mother who is living with relatives in an extended family. The presence of the husband had no relation to child survival. This suggests that children in households headed by women will not be less likely to survive.

The schooling variable functioned as expected: More-educated women had fewer deceased children and tended to have fewer children overall (also reported by LeVine in this volume). But work status also had an independent relationship with child survival in this sample, controlling for maternal schooling history. Thus, job status, as measured here, is not simply a measure of education. It is possible that the work variable serves as a proxy for level of energy, good health, or competence, as well as for increased income. In these villages, one observes that women in apparently similar economic circumstances differ considerably in how they approach the world. Some are energetic and enthusiastic and respected by their peers, whereas other women seem passive, burdened, and lacking in energy.

Although in this analysis the *working* measure was a report of the mother's current status, it may also reflect an underlying tendency to work, but current work status does not necessarily reflect the mother's activities at the time of the birth of her children. Theoretically, working either before or after a child's birth could influence the child's survival. Working before a baby is born might lead to less adequate fetal nutrition because of the mother's overexpenditure of energy, and work during the interval after the birth of a child might result in a shorter breastfeeding time and in reduction of childcare time spent with the infant.

In this data set, it was possible to examine the relationship of reported work in the interval preceding birth to the outcome of that birth, as well as the influence of work in the interval following the birth on the outcome. These analyses were performed at the level of the individual child.

No associations were found between a baby's survival and the mother's report of work performed either before or after the baby was born. This finding is not surprising, since 84 percent of infants who die do so in the first week, before a reduction in maternal care time because of employment can be presumed to operate. Also, for this sample working may not be related to shorter breastfeeding times. *T*-tests comparing the length of lactation of working and nonworking mothers of surviving babies were not significant ($t = -.62$, $df = 210$). Moreover, only 2.2 percent of women who reported lactating less than a year (a short period) indicated that maternal employment was a factor limiting breastfeeding.

The lack of association between house quality and either (1) proportion of children who survive or (2) number of deceased children was unexpected. One explanation may be that the economic variables having greatest impact on infant survival, such as diet and health care, may be more related to the mother than to permanent investment in the house. Money is crucial to daily survival in these villages; Balderston and others (1981) report that 70 percent of the families in these four villages supplemented the income they received from farming. Between 35 and 54 percent of the families' income comes from nonfarm sources. Thus, the extra income that a woman can generate through her occupation may make a critical difference in the food and the health care that she can provide for her children. Sharman (1970) has noted that, in marginal situations, small differences in the allocation of income can have large effects on children's health and nutritional status. In support of this point, Wilson (1981) found that in the four villages of our Guatemalan study children of mothers with occupations had significantly better home diets at eighteen and thirty months, even controlling for a number of other variables, such as parental literacy, than did the children of nonworking mothers. He reported no relationship between a factor score assessing house quality and the quality of the child's home diet. Thus, the quality of the diet and the long-term survival and nutritional status of the child may be more directly related to the mother's income than to overall family wealth as measured by house quality. The differential effect of mothers' income, as opposed to fathers' income, for child welfare is also indicated by Wilson's analyses. Fathers' occupations were unrelated to children's home diets at ages eighteen and thirty months and negatively related to children's home diets at forty-two months. This interpretation would be consistent with Blumberg's (1981) hypothesis that women use their income for family welfare. She states that "increasing the proportion of a class's resources in the hands of its females will have a rapid and more immediate consequence for the level of individual well-being than comparable increases in the hands of its males" (p. 40).

These findings suggest that the loss of maternal time because of involvement in income-generating activities is more than offset by the increased income available to the mother. They are also consistent with findings that, when women have adequate income either through full-time work or regular factory work, the nutritional status of their children can be adequate (see also Wray and Aguirre, 1969, in Colombia; Haggerty, 1981, in Haiti).

Conclusions

In traditional rural villages in Guatemala, children of working mothers were more likely to survive than children of nonworking women. Child survival was greater in nuclear than in extended families when the mother had more schooling and when she reported current work. House quality and marital status were unrelated to child survival. Extrapolating from the model initially proposed, the results suggest that (controlling for maternal education and wealth) increased income associated with work has a more powerful impact on child survival than the probable decrease in childcare time does. Whether a woman worked, either before or after a child's birth, was generally unrelated to child survival.

There is a need for more research in this area. Few studies exist and samples are small, but the few available data are being used by policy makers. This chapter suggests that maternal work may have a positive impact on child survival; the mechanism may be increased income available to the mother, which then is reflected in improved diet for the family. This finding underscores Blumberg's (1981) hypothesis that development efforts should support women's control over resources and means of production so as to enhance the well-being of children.

What is the future of women's work and of child welfare in developing countries? All indications suggest that women's work roles will become more prevalent and more visible in the coming years (Nieves, 1981). In our sample, 64 percent of the women indicated that they would like to work more (Engle, 1982), and most saw other obligations or their husbands' opinions, rather than the presence of children, as the major obstacles. Childcare may become more of a problem as these work patterns change, because there may be fewer older siblings and grandmothers available for alternative childcare. Intervention studies, designed both to improve women's wage-earning ability and to examine the effects of these improvements on child welfare and survival, should be undertaken as soon as possible.

References

Abbott, J. "The Employment of Women and the Reduction of Fertility: Implications for Development." *World Development,* 1974, *2* (2), 23-26.

Acharya, M. "Time-Use Data and the Living Standards Measurement Study." Working paper no. 18. Washington, D.C.: World Bank, 1982.

Alfonja, S. "Changing Modes of Production and the Sexual Division of Labor Among the Yoruba." *Signs: Journal of Women in Culture and Society,* 1981, *7* (2), 299-313.

Balderston, J. B., Wilson, A. B., Freire, M., and Simonen, M. *Malnourished Children of the Rural Poor.* Boston: Auburn, 1981.

Battad, J. P. "Determinants of Nutritional Status of Preschoolers." *Philippine Economic Journal,* 1978, *36* (17), 154-167.

Behrman, J. R., and Wolfe, B. L. "The Impact of Health and Nutrition on the Number of Surviving Children in a Developing Metropolis." Mimeo, 1979.

Benería, L., and Sen, G. "Accumulation, Reproduction, and Women's Role in Economic Development: Boserup Revisited." *Signs: Journal of Women in Culture and Society,* 1981, *7* (2), 279-298.

Bittencourt, S. "Child Care Needs of Low-Income Women: Urban Brazil." Washington, D.C.: Overseas Education Fund, 1979.

Bloch, M. N. "Maternal Employment, Substitute Caretakers, and the Social Behavior of Senegalese Preschool Age Children." Paper presented at the American Educational Research Association Meeting, Toronto, March 1978.

Blumberg, R. L. "Rural Women in Development." In M. Black and A. B. Cottrell, *Women and World Change.* Beverly Hills: Sage, 1981.

Boserup, E. *Women's Role in Economic Development.* New York: St. Martin's Press, 1970.

Cabañero, T. A. "The 'Shadow Price' of Children in Laguna Households." *Philippine Economic Journal,* 1978, *36,* 62-87.

Cain, M., Khanam, S., and Nahar, S. "Class Patriarchy and the Structure of Women's Work in Rural Bangladesh." Center for Policy Studies working paper no. 43. New York: The Population Council, 1979.

Chaudhury, R. H. "Married Women in Urban Occupations of Bangladesh: Some Problems and Issues." Paper presented at Conference on Women and Development, Wellesley College, June 1976.

Chavez, M. L., and Loucky, J. "Caretaking and Competence: Siblings as Socializers in Rural Guatemala." *Anthropology UCLA,* 1981, *11* (1, 2), 1-23.

Cherry, F. F., and Eaton, E. L. "Physical and Cognitive Development in Children of Low-Income Mothers Working in the Child's Early Years." *Child Development,* 1977, *48,* 158-166.

Clark, C. "Women's Work and Infant Nutrition." Paper presented at the *Seminario latinoamericano sobre interrelación de nutrición, población y desarollo social y enónico,* Antigua, Guatemala, September 1979.

Cochrane, S. H. "Fertility and Education: What Do We Really Know?" World Bank staff occasional paper no. 26. Washington, D.C.: World Bank, 1979.

DaVanzo, J., and Butz, W. P. "Birthspacing, Fertility, and Family Planning: Policy and Program Implications from the Malaysian Family Life Survey." The RAND Corporation, 1981.

DaVanzo, J., and Lee, D. L. P. "The Compatibility of Child Care with Labor Force Participation and Non-Market Activities: Preliminary Evidence from Malaysian Time Budget Data." Paper presented at the ICRW conference on women in poverty, Washington, D.C., May 1978.

Engle, P. L. "The Intersecting Needs of Working Mothers and Their Children." Report to the Ford Foundation, August 1980.

Engle, P. L. "Discrepancy Between Guatemalan Women's Desire to Work and Actual Employment." Paper presented at research conference of the Center for the Study, Education, and Advancement of Women, Berkeley, May 1982.

Engle, P. L., Yarbrough, C., Townsend, J., and Klein, R. E. "Sex Differences in the Effects of Nutrition and Social Environment on Mental Development in Rural Guatemala." In M. Lycette and W. P. McGreevey (Eds.), *Women and Poverty.* Baltimore: Johns Hopkins Press, in press.

Evanson, R. E. "Introduction." *Philippine Economic Journal,* 1978, *17,* 1-31.

Fagley, R. M. *Rural Women as Food Producers: Initial Responses to a Recent Questionnaire.* New York: Commission of the Churches on International Affairs, 1975.

Fagley, R. M. "Easing the Burden of Women: The Sixteen-Hour Workday." *Assignment Children,* 1976, No. 36, entire issue.

Germain, A. "Status and Roles of Women as Factors in Fertility Behavior: A Policy Analysis." *Studies in Family Planning,* 1975, *6* (7), 192-200.

Greiner, T. H. "Breastfeeding in Decline—Perspectives on the Causes." In D. B. Jelliffe, E. F. P. Jelliffe, F. T. Sai, and P. Senanayake (Eds.), *Lactation, Fertility, and the Working Woman.* London: International Planned Parenthood Federation, 1979.

Habicht, J. P. "Public Health Implications of Present Evidence for Long-Term Behavioral Consequences of Energy and Protein Deficits." In J. Brozek (Ed.), *Behavioral*

Effects of Energy and Protein Deficits. Washington, D.C.: U.S. Department of Health, Education, and Welfare, 1977.

Haggerty, P. A. "Women's Work in Child Nutrition in Haiti." Unpublished masters thesis, Massachusetts Institute of Technology, Cambridge, 1981.

Ho, T. "Time Costs of Child-Rearing in Rural Philippines." *Population and Development Review,* 1979, *5,* 643-662.

Hoffman, L. W. "Maternal Employment: 1979." *American Psychologist,* 1979, *34,* 859-865.

International Center for Research on Women (ICRW). "Keeping Women Out: A Structural Analysis of Women's Employment in Developing Countries." Paper prepared for AID by International Center for Research on Women, 1980.

Jelliffe, E. F. P. "Breastfeeding and the Working Woman—Bending the Rules." In D. B. Jelliffe, E. F. P. Jelliffe, F. T. Sai, and P. Senanayake (Eds.), *Lactation, Fertility, and the Working Woman.* London: International Planned Parenthood Federation, 1979.

Kumar, S. K. "Composition of Economic Constraints in Child Nutrition: Impact of Maternal Incomes and Employment in Low-Income Households." Unpublished doctoral dissertation, Cornell University, 1977.

LeVine, R. A. "A Cross-Cultural Perspective on Parenting." In M. Fantini and R. Cardenas, (Eds.), *Parenting in a Multicultural Society.* New York: Longman, 1980.

Levinson, F. S. "Morinda: An Economic Analysis of Malnutrition Among Young Children in Rural India." Cornell-MIT International Nutrition Policy Series, 1974.

Maccan, S. Z., and Bamberger, M. "The Effects of Employment and Education on the Status of Women in Venezuela: A Progress Report." Paper presented at the Eighth World Congress of the Committee on Family Research, International Sociological Association, August 1974.

McGuire, J. "Seasonal Changes in Energy Expenditure and Work Patterns of Rural Guatemalan Women." Unpublished doctoral dissertation, Massachusetts Institute of Technology, 1979.

Mejía Piveral, V. "Características económicas y socioculturales de cuatro aldeas Ladinas de Guatemala. *Guatemala Indígena,* 1972, *8* (3), entire issue.

Nerlove, S. B., Roberts, J. M., Klein, R. E., Yarbrough, D. S., and Habicht, J. P. "Natural Indicators of Cognitive Development: An Observational Study of Rural Guatemalan Children." *Ethos,* 1974, *2,* 265-295.

Nieves, I. "A Balancing Act: Strategies to Cope with Work and Motherhood in Developing Countries." Background paper prepared for International Center for Research on Women's Round Table, December 10, 1981.

Popkin, B. "Women, Work, and Child Welfare." Paper presented at the Women in Poverty conference, May 1978.

Popkin, B. M., and Solon, F. S. "Income, Time, the Working Mother, and Child Nutrition." *Journal of Tropical Pediatrics and Environmental Child Health,* 1976, *22,* 156-166.

Reining, P., Camara, F., Chinas, B., Fanale, R., Gojman de Millan, S., Lenkerd, B., Shinohara, I., and Tinker, I. *Village Women, Their Changing Lives and Fertility: Studies in Kenya, Mexico, and the Philippines.* American Association for the Advancement of Science, Washington, D.C., 1977.

Riccuiti, H. N. "Malnutrition and Cognitive Development: Research Issues and Priorities." In J. Brozek (Ed.), *Behavioral Effects of Energy and Protein Deficits.* Washington, D.C.: U.S. Department of Health, Education, and Welfare, 1977.

Rivera, C. M. "Labor Force Participation and Day Care Utilization by Low-Income Mothers in Bogota, Colombia." Unpublished doctoral dissertation, Brandeis University, 1979.

Safilios-Rothschild, C. "The Role of the Family: A Neglected Aspect of Poverty." World Development Report. Washington, D.C.: World Bank, 1980.

Sharman, A. "Nutrition and Social Planning." *People, Planning, and Developmental Studies,* 1970, *6,* 77–91.

Stavrakis, O., and Marshall, S. M. L. "Women, Agriculture, and Development in the Maya Lowlands: Profit or Progress?" Presented at the International Conference on Women and Food, University of Arizona, Tucson, 1978.

Taylor, C., and others. *Malnutrition and Infection in Weaning-Age Punjabi Children.* Ludhiana, India: Rural Health Research Center, 1971.

Tripp, R. B. "Farmers and Traders: Some Economic Determinants of Nutritional Status in Northern Ghana." *Journal of Tropical Pediatrics and Environmental Child Health,* 1981, *27,* 15–22.

Weisner, T. S., and Gallimore, R. "My Brother's Keeper: Child and Sibling Caretaking." *Current Anthropology,* 1977, *18* (2), 169–190.

Wilson, A. B. "Longitudinal Analyses of Diet, Physical Growth, Verbal Development, and School Performance." In J. B. Balderston, A. B. Wilson, M. Freire, and M. Simonen, *Malnourished Children of the Rural Poor.* Boston: Auburn, 1981.

Wray, J. D., and Aguirre, A. "Protein-Calorie Malnutrition in Candelaria, Colombia. I. Prevalence: Social and Demographic Causal Factors." *Journal of Tropical Pediatrics,* 1969, *25,* 76.

Patricia L. Engle is assistant professor of child development at California Polytechnic State University in San Luis Obispo, California. She has been studying the effects of nutrition, social stimulation, and family demography on children's mental development in Latin America for a number of years and has published on the effects of maternal income generation on family functioning and children's welfare. Her field experience includes research and program development in Latin America and research on Latin women's responses to health care in the United States.

Indigenous school systems often feature literacy as a central focus, but such systems have generally been ignored by development planners.

Indigenous Education and Literacy in the Third World

Daniel A. Wagner

The current world economic crisis had led most nations to reconsider the need as well as priorities for social and material well-being. For these nations, and particularly for Third World countries, budgets for educational institutions and for educational instruction are at the top of the list of costs. Thus, it should not be surprising that such countries are beginning to reassess the utility and productivity of educational programs in light of current economic changes. While a number of specialists have questioned the basic premise that education and functional literacy are primary forces behind labor productivity and economic development (Silvey, in press; Simmons, 1979), others have chosen to promote alternative, nonformal educational programs as more cost-effective for Third World settings (Coombs, Prosser, and Ahmed, 1973).

Within the sphere of options just mentioned for teaching and learning, the present chapter will develop three themes:

1. Alternative, indigenous forms of schooling are potentially important national resources in many Third World countries, but have generally been ignored by development planners.

The author would like to acknowledge the important contribution of Abdelhamid Lotfi in undertaking comparative research in the Islamic countries mentioned in this chapter. Support for this research was provided in part by grants from the Ford Foundation, Social Science Research Council, International Development Research Centre, the Spencer Foundation, NIE (#80-0182), and NIH (#HD-14898).

2. Literacy instruction has often been a central feature, and literacy acquisition a frequent product, of indigenous school systems.

3. National literacy programs and policies in the Third World, as in many industrialized nations, have achieved only limited success in recent decades and could benefit considerably from a closer relationship with extant and culturally indigenous forms of teaching and learning.

The suggestion that indigenous education should be counted among the natural resources of a society parallels the Darwinian argument that the probability of survival is greatest where there is a diversity of specialized adaptations. That is, with more educational and literacy opportunities available in a given society, the specific individual or group is more likely to find an appropriate cultural, linguistic, or religious niche in which to learn useful skills. Recent research on traditional Islamic schooling, a system that has survived for centuries despite adverse circumstances, demonstrates this point. Islamic schooling will also serve here to illustrate the importance of indigenous education for millions of children, and possibly for national development programs as well, in the coming years.

Indigenous Education and Islamic Schools

Indigenous education is defined here as any formalized (that is, culturally codified, recognized, or authorized) system of instruction that is not a direct descendant of modern public schooling, which developed in Europe during the Renaissance. Prior to the Renaissance, most formalized education in the world would also have been termed *indigenous*, since it was rooted in culturally and historically adapted practices. During the colonial period of the seventeenth to the twentieth centuries, European education was exported to many Third World nations, where it came into contact and occasional conflict with indigenous educational systems. These surviving indigenous systems generally have been overlooked in the rush to modernize and Westernize education in the Third World.

Pre-Renaissance formal European schooling generally took the form of religious instruction and made use of traditional pedagogical methods. In Christian as well as Jewish schools, the focus was on memorizing sacred texts during lengthy periods of study with a single teacher. The early years of study emphasized rote learning, while later years included in-depth understanding of texts through the student's apprenticeship to a given master. Students were not age-graded as in post-Renaissance school classrooms but, rather, learned a set of required texts through a tutorial process in which the teacher provided tasks as a function of student's abilities and accomplishments (Wagner, in press; Wagner and Lotfi, 1980). Such traditional methods are remarkably similar to those discussed in recent research trends (concerning adult and cross-age tutoring) in the study of cognitive potential in children (Greenfield and Lave, 1982; Vygotsky, 1978; Wood, Bruner, and Ross, 1974). In addition, such schooling provided "cultural capital" (Bourdieu, 1973; Eickelman,

1978), in terms of a body of knowledge important for the child's successful functioning in the society as well as for future social status.

While European traditional education has declined dramatically over the centuries (with some important exceptions, such as the Jewish *yeshiva* schools, see Roskies, 1978), indigenous education and traditional pedagogy can still be found in many parts of the Third World. Buddhist traditional pedagogy exhibits many parallels with the European examples (see Gurugé, in press; Tambiah, 1968, on Thailand; or Yoo, 1958, on Korea). African bush schools, such as those described by Gay (1973) in Liberia, involve the memorization of oral rather than written texts and result in similar acquisition of cultural capital. Because of its longevity, prevalence, and geographical and cultural diversity, the most widespread example of indigenous education and traditional pedagogy in the contemporary world seems to be Islamic education.

Curiously, Islamic, or Quranic, schools are also among the least-studied educational institutions in the contemporary world, even though millions of children in dozens of countries attend such schools for either part or all of their formal education. In a recent comparative study of Islamic schooling in Indonesia, Yemen, Senegal, Morocco, and Egypt, we (Wagner, 1982; Wagner and Lotfi, 1983) found considerable diversity in these schools, both across societies and within societies. In spite of their emphasis on the study of Quranic texts, which provides a similar focus for Islamic schooling across the world, Quranic schools have adapted to a number of cultural constraints within each society. For example, Islamic schooling in Indonesia (which, with over 100 million Muslims, is the world's most populous Islamic society, and which sends over 20 million children to Islamic schools each year) was overlaid on and still maintains some of the features of an earlier Buddhist system, including a long-term apprenticeship and the attribution of mystical powers to the religious teacher. By contrast, most children in North Yemen go through only three to five years of Quranic schooling, and the Quranic teacher, beyond instructing children, often serves as a legal arbiter in his village because he is a literate person who can read documents to adjudicate legal disputes (Messick, 1983).

Also important is the fact that Quranic schools vary dramatically even within societies, primarily as a function of the last several decades of modernization. In Morocco, where about 90 percent of all children now attend Quranic schools, the traditional schools for older children are disappearing, while the modernized Quranic schools, which sometimes employ teachers with public high school diplomas, are attracting more young children than ever before. One important reason for this increase in attendance is the participation of girls, who were once excluded from such schools. In Senegal, where girls traditionally have attended the Quranic schools, modernization has led to significant changes in pedagogy and curriculum. Rather than emphasizing rote learning of Arabic texts, which are not understood by children who speak only Senegalese languages, many Quranic school teachers are now trying to teach spoken and written Arabic as a second language. Changes such as those found in Morocco and Senegal are taking place in many parts of the Islamic world, as people adapt to changing societal pressures. These changes have also placed Quranic schooling in more direct competition with the modern secular school systems of many Muslim societies, since the modernized Quranic schools now provide a culturally and religiously valued alternative with fewer of the drawbacks of the traditional pedagogies (see also Brown and Hiskett, 1975; Wagner, in press).

This brief description of contemporary Islamic education provides one important example of indigenous education in today's world. The Islamic school system, which remained relatively static over many centuries, has now begun to undergo significant changes, which vary from society to society. The point to be emphasized here is that Islamic schools, like other indigenous schools, continue to attract large—indeed, enormous—numbers of children, many of whom never attend governmental secular schools. Clearly, such indigenous schools are both a natural and a national resource for those who would try to reach the rural poor in societies split between the elites of the city and the poor of the countryside.

Literacy Instruction in Modern and Indigenous Schools

The achievement of literacy has been, perhaps, the only area of complete curricular agreement among contemporary educational systems. Often defined simply as the individual's possession of and control of the skills of reading and writing, literacy nevertheless has been studied by specialists who consider its acquisition to be both an individual and a social phenomenon. More recently, literacy has been studied increasingly in its historical and social contexts (Clanchy, 1979; Goody, 1968; Graff, 1979; Oxenham, 1980). In addition, as noted earlier, literacy has been suggested as a factor crucial to promoting economic development (Anderson and Bowman, 1966; Harman, 1974; Lerner, 1958). In the modern educational sector, literacy is usually considered to be one of the products of the standard curriculum; for this reason, national and international organizations typically calculate the percent of literate persons in each country from the number of children and adults who have attended at least four years of elementary school. In some cases this figure is a clear overestimation of national literacy, since schooling may be poor, attendance low, or retention minimal (see Freire, 1970; Noesjirwan, 1974; Simmons, 1976). In other cases, literacy may be underestimated, as when those who calculate national literacy rates fail to consider that literacy is often acquired in indigenous schools (see Wagner and Lotfi, 1983).

The first major collection of work on literacy acquisition in indigenous schools was the volume by Goody (1968), which included a significant section on Islamic school literacy. In our own research and in the work of others (Ferguson, 1971; Jurmo, 1980; O'Halloran, 1979; Scribner and Cole, 1981), literacy instruction has been shown to be an important product of Quranic schooling, but also one that may vary substantially across teachers, schools, and societies. Disregarding, for the moment, the modernization changes noted in the previous discussion, a traditional Quranic school includes a number of common features for literacy instruction: oral memorization of the Quran; emphasis on correct (that is, accurate and aesthetic) oral recitation; training in the Arabic script; and strict authoritarian instruction. In contrast to the primers used in virtually all modern public schools, literacy instruction with the Quran as its text provides no opportunity for age-graded vocabulary or grammatical structures. In addition, the picture captions that most primers use to facilitate reading are strictly prohibited for religious reasons in Islamic schools.

Although we know that literacy acquisition takes place in Islamic schools, we still lack firm statistics on the actual degree of literacy accomplishment among children in any single society. (A four-year project we are currently conducting in Morocco, however, will help shed light on this issue; for more details, wee Wagner and others, in press). The key question here is probably not the exact degree of reading and writing skill possessed by the child but, rather, the relationship between levels of literacy skills and the uses to which the skills are or may be put. This argument was promulgated by UNESCO's Experimental World Literacy Program (1976), in which the term *functional literacy* was suggested as a way of defining national and international goals of literacy promotion. The term was never adequately defined, however (for a critique, see Anzalone, 1981), and the culturally and historically valued functions and uses of literacy are only now being adequately explored (Heath, 1980; Reder and Green, 1983). This generalization is particularly true with respect to those Third World nations where a relatively small percentage of the population plays an active role in the modern sector of society and where literacy is most often acquired in indigenous schools. In the modern sector, literacy is primarily defined by the standard uses of reading for information acquisition and of writing for information transmission; in traditional settings, literacy can be defined in part through its utility for social and religious powerbrokers, traditional medicine and amulets, and simple commercial accounting (Scribner and Cole, 1981).

In the case of contemporary Islamic schools, we can raise two reasonable questions about the functional utility of Arabic literacy acquired through Quranic study. First, can religious literacy be transferred in a meaningful way to secular societal tasks? There is some evidence that it can be in the Christian (Reder and Green, 1983), Jewish (Spolsky, 1983), and Islamic (Wagner and others, in press) traditions, although more evidence surely needs to be gathered. Second, of what use is literacy in Arabic for the majority of the world's Muslims, who are not native Arabic speakers? Such literacy acquisition in Arabic is certainly more difficult for non-native speakers (for a review, see Engle, 1975), and yet there remains considerable skepticism about the possibility of teaching literacy skills in each child's vernacular tongue (Heyneman,

1980). It is true that, in contrast to the typical case of imposing a European language on a multilingual colonial society, Arabic literacy has the advantage of being already firmly embedded in the cultural fabric of societies with significant Muslim populations. At the present time, however, the choice of the national language of literacy and of public school instruction remains a political one.

While these and other questions cause difficulties in policy planning for literacy, we need to bear in mind the fact that, for many children, literacy skills are acquired in indigenous schools rather than in government-run schools. In addition, in many societies the functions of literacy cannot and should not be uniquely defined by modern economic planners, since many indigenous literacies have histories that go back several centuries and are likely to continue well into the future. Rather than viewing indigenous education and indigenous literacies as impediments to their policies, national development planners should consider such literacies as resources. To reiterate, the reality is that, for a substantial portion of the world's children, literacy skills are acquired in indigenous rather than in government-run schools.

Policy Implications from Research on Indigenous Education and Literacy in the Third World

Literacy in general, and in the Third World, is often perceived as something that can be achieved once and for always. Campaigns have been waged to "eradicate illiteracy" in much the same way that we have eradicated smallpox, by a quick cure akin to inoculation. It is now well documented that such literacy programs have achieved only limited success (Anzalone, 1981; IDRC, 1979). Moreover, illiteracy has not been eradicated; rather, it has increased in the Third World, as well as in such industrialized societies as the United States (see Hunter and Harman, 1979). Rather than focusing on the factors that led to program failures, the discussion here has attempted to describe successful literacy acquisition as it currently exists in many Third World countries, and which has usually been ignored by foreign and local policy makers alike.

Indigenous education and indigenous literacy training have existed for centuries. While some indigenous educational systems have declined over the years, others—such as Islamic schooling—have maintained important cultural roles and reach more children today than they did in the past. The development of modern educational methods and institutions in the Third World is often viewed as a key variable in promoting economic growth. Still, the present situation suggests that there may be a lack of fit between modern educational methods and indigenous schooling as it exists in traditional and developing societies. It is incumbent upon us to be better informed about existing cultural competencies so that we can avoid wasting financial resources through program failure while we simultaneously take advantage of already available cultural resources. In this way, even in the present world economic crisis, development planners and policy makers may be able either to increase literacy or simply make use of it in areas where indigenous schooling touches the lives of many children and where public secular schooling has been ineffective. Nevertheless, cultural and, in particular, religious traditions have a long history of resisting attempts at cooptation and abuse by outsiders. Implementation of some of the ideas presented here would require a significant effort to establish rapport and mutual respect between planners and those individuals responsible for the integrity and maintenance of traditional practices.

References

Anderson, C. A., and Bowman, M. J. *Education and Economic Development.* London: Frank Cass, 1966.
Anzalone, S. J. "Why Can't Abu Read? A Critique of Modern Literacy Doctrine." Unpublished doctoral dissertation, University of Massachusetts, 1981.
Bourdieu, P. "Cultural Reproduction and Social Reproduction." In R. Brown (Ed.), *Knowledge, Education, and Social Change.* London: Tavistock, 1973.
Brown, G., and Hiskett, M. *Conflict and Harmony in Education in Tropical Africa.* London: Allen & Unwin, 1975.
Clanchy, M. T. *From Memory to Written Records: England, 1066-1307.* Cambridge, Mass.: Harvard University Press, 1979.
Coombs, P. H., Prosser, R. C., and Ahmed, M. *New Paths to Learning for Rural Children and Youth.* New York: International Council for Educational Development, 1973.
Eickelman, D. "The Art of Memory: Islamic Education and Its Social Reproduction." *Comparative Studies in Society and History,* 1978, *20,* 485-516.
Engle, P. "The Uses of Vernacular Languages in Education." *Review of Educational Research,* 1975, *45,* 283-325.
Ferguson, C. A. "Contrasting Patterns of Literacy Acquisition in a Multilingual Nation." In W. H. Whiteley (Ed.), *Language Use and Social Change.* London: International African Institute, 1971.
Freire, P. *Pedagogy of the Oppressed.* New York: Herder & Herder, 1970.
Gay, J. *Red Dust on Green Leaves.* Thompson, Conn.: InterCultural Association, 1973.
Goody, J. *Literacy in Traditional Societies.* Cambridge, England: Cambridge University Press, 1968.
Graff, H. *The Literacy Myth.* New York: Academic Press, 1979.
Greenfield, P., and Lave, J. "Cognitive Aspects of Informal Education." In D. A. Wagner and H. W. Stevenson (Eds.), *Cultural Perspectives on Child Development.* San Francisco: W. H. Freeman, 1982.
Gurugé, A. "Buddhist Education." In T. Husen and T. N. Postlethwaite (Eds.), *International Encyclopedia of Education: Research and Studies.* New York: Pergamon Press, in press.
Harman, D. *Community Fundamental Education.* Lexington, Mass.: D. C. Heath, 1974.
Heath, S. "The Functions and Uses of Literacy." *Journal of Communication,* 1980, *30,* 123-133.
Heyneman, S. "Instruction in the Mother Tongue: The Question of Logistics." *Canadian and International Education,* 1980, *9,* 88-94.
Hunter, S. S. J., and Harman, D. *Adult Illiteracy in the United States.* New York: McGraw-Hill, 1979.

International Development Research Centre (IDRC). *The World of Literacy: Research, Policy, Action.* Ottawa: IDRC, 1979.

Jurmo, P. "The Use of Traditional Stories in Literacy Work." Paper presented at symposium titled "A New Look at Literacy," University of Massachusetts, Amherst, July 1980.

Lerner, D. *The Passing of Traditional Society.* New York: Free Press, 1958.

Messick, B. "Legal Documents and the Concept of 'Restricted Literacy' in a Traditional Society." *International Journal of the Sociology of Language,* 1983, *42,* 41–52.

Noesjirwan, J. "Permanency of Literacy in Indonesia." *American Educational Research Journal,* 1974, *11,* 93–99.

O'Halloran, G. "Indigenous Literacy Among the Mandinko of West Africa." *Journal of Reading,* 1979, *22* (6), 492–497.

Oxenham, J. *Literacy: Writing, Reading, and Social Organization.* London: Routledge & Kegan Paul, 1980.

Reder, S., and Green, K. "Contrasting Patterns of Literacy in an Alaskan Fishing Village." *International Journal of the Sociology of Language,* 1983, *42,* 9–39.

Roskies, D. "Alphabet Instruction in the East European Heder: Some Comparative and Historical Notes." *YIVO Annual of Jewish Social Studies,* 1978, *17.*

Scribner, S., and Cole, M. *The Psychology of Literacy.* Cambridge, Mass.: Harvard University Press, 1981.

Silvey, J. "Recent Developments in Educational Selection Methods in Third World Nations." In J. W. Berry and S. Irvine (Eds.), *Human Assessment and Cultural Factors.* New York: Plenum, in press.

Simmons, J. "Retention of Cognitive Skills Acquired in Primary School." *Comparative Education Review,* 1976, *20,* 79–93.

Simmons, J. "Education for Development, Reconsidered." *World Development,* 1979, *7,* 1005–1016.

Spolsky, B. "Jewish Literacy in the First Century." *International Journal of the Sociology of Language,* 1983, *42,* 95–110.

Tambiah, S. J. "Literacy in a Buddhist Village in North-East Thailand." In J. Goody (Ed.), *Literacy in Traditional Societies.* Cambridge, England: Cambridge University Press, 1968.

UNESCO. *The Experimental World Literacy Program: A Critical Assessment.* Paris: UNESCO/UNDP, 1976.

Vygotsky, L. *Mind in Society.* Cambridge, Mass.: Harvard University Press, 1978.

Wagner, D. A. "Quranic Lessons." *Arabia: The Islamic World Review,* 1982, *16,* 69–70.

Wagner, D. A. "Islamic Education: Traditional Pedagogy and Contemporary Change." In T. Husen and T. N. Postlethwaite (Eds.), *International Encyclopedia of Education: Research and Studies.* New York: Pergamon Press, in press.

Wagner, D. A., and Lotfi, A. "Traditional Islamic Education in Morocco." *Comparative Education Review,* 1980, *24,* 238–251.

Wagner, D. A., and Lotfi, A. "Learning to Read by 'Rote.'" *International Journal of the Sociology of Language,* 1983, *42,* 111–121.

Wagner, D. A., Messick, B. M., Spratt, J., and Seeley, K. M. "Studying Literacy in Morocco." In B. B. Schieffelin (Ed.), *The Acquisition of Literacy: Ethnographic Perspectives.* Norwood, N.J.: Ablex, in press.

Wood, D., Bruner, J. S., and Ross, G. "The Role of Tutoring in Problem Solving." *Journal of Child Psychology and Psychiatry,* 1974, *17,* 89–100.

Yoo, H. J. "An Intellectual History of Korea from Ancient Times to the Impact of the West with Special Emphasis upon Education." Unpublished doctoral dissertation, Harvard University, 1958.

Daniel A. Wagner is associate professor of human development in the Graduate School of Education, University of Pennsylvania. He is primarily interested in child development in the Third World and is currently involved in a four-year research project on the acquisition and maintenance of literacy in Morocco. With Harold W. Stenvenson, he edited Cultural Perspectives on Child Development *(Freeman, 1982).*

This chapter provides an introduction to and a bibliography on the issue of child labor and its relationship to economic development in the Third World.

Child Labor and National Development: An Annotated Bibliography

Elizabeth B. Moore

Child labor is an issue that has recently gained attention as a phenomenon common to many Third World countries. Researchers dealing with child employment have used a number of different approaches and methodologies. There are those who see it as a purely economic phenomenon (Mueller, 1976; Rosenzweig, 1981; Vlassoff, 1979) or as a stage in economic development (Nagi, 1972). Some scholars analyze the socioeconomic value of the child in a given society (Mueller, 1976; Repetto, 1976; Tienda, 1979). There are also those who view child labor as a political question concerning those governments that are reluctant to enforce existing legislation (Porter, 1975; Anti-Slavery Society, 1978). The phenonemon has been connected to the class structure of society by some scholars (Morice, 1981) and to the prevailing mode of production in society by others (Rodgers and Standing, 1981a, 1981b; Hull, 1981). In addition, some analytical case studies integrating several of these approaches have been produced (Chan, 1975; Cain, 1977; De la Luz Silva, 1981).

Beyond such socioeconomic analyses, child labor has as yet been addressed only superficially with respect to its effect on the child's psychological development. Most authors limit their discussions primarily to physical effects on the child and do not attempt to place child labor within the context of psychological or anthropological theory. What effect does a child's early entrance into the labor market have upon his or her cognitive and social development? How are sex roles socialized with respect to child employment? Is child work a cultural process common to all societies, one that inculcates adult values and norms? Also, how are Western views of child labor shaped by particular cultural paradigms, which in turn are influenced by Western economic and social development? Given the lack of relevant research, these kinds of questions are only peripherally dealt with in the annotated bibliography that follows.

According to most of the authors reviewed here, there are a number of reasons why it is difficult both to gauge the number of children who work throughout the world and to estimate the impact of child employment on the global economy. First, there is the problem of defining the terms *child, work,* and *child labor*. Second, the problem of definition is related to the prevailing paradigms and methodological tools used by most analysts to measure the extent of child work in a given society. Ambiguous definitions, of course, mean that statistics gathered on the phenomenon are frequently inaccurate or invalid. In addition, there are the political and social ramifications of estimating child labor, which may alter the official statistics. This chapter, then, consists of two sections. The first section provides a summary of key definitions in this research area; the second section is an annotated bibliography of the research literature on child labor, with particular emphasis on the Third World.

Definitions

The Child. Until recently, many authors defined *child* according to biological age: A child was a preadolescent or adolescent individual under fourteen or fifteen who needed adult nurturance, guidance, and protection until he or she reached physical, social, emotional, and intellectual maturity. Although considered universal, this definition was in fact shaped by a change in Western social attitudes toward children and child work. This change occurred within a few generations, as a result of the economic and demographic changes brought about by the Industrial Revolution. In their reviews of the history of childhood in the West, Aries (1962), Plumb (1980), and De Mause (1974) demonstrate that only in the last few hundred years have children been considered anything except miniature adults with adult obligations, needs, and tastes. Prior to the Industrial Revolution, "there was no special word [in English, French, or German] for a young man between the ages of seven and sixteen; the word 'child' expressed kinship, not an age state" (Plumb, p. 17). Aries has pointed out that the chronological method of calculating age is a relatively recent phenomenon in the West and is partly the result of a formal educational system structured according to annual age grades. In non-Western societies, the use of chronological age in defining a child is particularly inappropriate because individuals are not always classified by calendars, recorded years, or dates of birth (Hull, 1981; Schildkrout, 1981).

Rodgers and Standing (1981a) support the supposition that childhood and chronological age were first linked primarily in industrialized societies. In preindustrial societies, there are instead socially and biologically defined stages, each of which involves a different degree of the child's dependence and a different set of obligations and behavior patterns. These patterns are sometimes distinguished by rites of passage, but at all times there is a gradual incorporation of the child into the adult world. Perhaps the most useful definition of the term *child* is provided by Beuf and Kurz (1980), who have considered the concept of childhood as a social construct and as a product of the social framework in which it is embedded. This interpretation helps to explain the "tremendous variations in the definition of childhood from one society to another and in the experiences of the child, which are rooted in the accepted definition" (p. 1).

Work. A definition of the term *work* is equally problematic. Some authors define work exclusively as paid labor. Because children are frequently not paid for their work, this criterion often results in a low statistical incidence of child labor. Many economists, such as Ridker (1976) and Mueller (1976), limit their definitions of work and economic activity to those activities that contribute to the gross national product. Thus, children working on family farms are considered workers, but those helping domestically are not considered workers, even if their work should help to release another family member for the labor market. In an effort to resolve the problem of defining work, De la Luz Silva (1981) suggests that work is "any socially useful, remunerable activity requiring manual and/or intellectual effort and conscious, purposeful action; that is, the production of a good or performance of a service." Accordingly, she distinguishes between work that promotes socialization (such as an apprenticeship) and other work. This other work can be classified additionally as conventional paid work (wage labor), unconventional paid work (prostitution), conventional unpaid work (domestic labor), and subsistence acts (begging). Schildkrout (1981) agrees that it is erroneous to equate work with pay: "Since children perform a great many tasks that are only indirectly linked to production and the generation of income, but which nonetheless have economic value, appraisal of their economic significance is only possible if the whole range of children's activities is considered, regardless of whether or not these activities fit our own ethnocentric definitions of work" (p. 95). Therefore, work must be defined in terms of the individual's sex, age, status, and sociocultural expectations.

Tienda (1979) is one of several economists who have challenged arbitrary definitions of the labor force. She states that "very general agreement on what constitutes economically productive activity hides serious conceptual ambiguity in the distinction of being classified as in or out of the labor force, particularly in those settings experiencing appreciable demographic or economic change" (p. 372). She argues for the adoption of a labor-use approach, which divides the labor force according to whether workers are adequately or inadequately used: Inadequate use, for example, is made of those actively seeking work as well as of those who are underused according to criteria of hours worked, level of income, and level of education. This definition is particularly appropriate in the Third World, where both underemployment of men and underuse of women distort the meaning of employment statistics.

Child Work and Child Labor. The most useful definition of children's work is supplied by Rodgers and Standing (1981a). They believe that children's roles as workers change according to the mode of production and the nature of the social system. In contrast to the situation of adults, for children work is not the main activity in most societies. Therefore, it is more useful to create a typology of children's activities, with classifications based on the nature of work performed and the time spent in working. These activities include domestic work, releasing adults into the workforce; nondomestic, nonmercenary work, usually in familial production, including agriculture; bonded labor, characteristic of feudal or semifeudal modes of production; wage labor, which can involve training in an apprenticeship, but can also be purely exploitative; marginal economic activities in the informal sector; schooling, which can be on a full-time or an intermittent basis; unemployment (especially after children have dropped out of school); recreational leisure; and reproductive activities, which the authors define as sleeping, eating, and other personal-care activities.

The problem of defining work is also related to the prevailing paradigms and methodological tools used by most analysts to measure the extent of children's work in a given society. The articles of Hull (1981), Morice (1981), and Rodgers and Standing (1981b) discuss inaccuracies and ambiguities in the statistics and definitions of many studies of children's work. In the past, most Western researchers were in agreement as to the evils of child labor, and few sought to examine its relationship to stages of economic development. By applying Western paradigms to non-Western phenomena, they misunderstood the complexity of children working in Third World societies and argued for its abolition. Children, however, do work out of socioeconomic necessity and because a given society sanctions the practice. Thus, child work will probably end only when either or both of these conditions are changed.

There are certain political and social ramifications of estimating child work and child labor, considerations that may call official governmental statistics into question. National governments, while they recognize the importance of child work, are also influenced by Western notions of child labor. Thus, they may abolish child labor legally, yet ignore it in reality by not including working children under the age of twelve in statistics or by failing to provide enough inspectors to control abusive practices.

A distinction also needs to be made between child work (defined as the child's participation in the family's economic life) and child labor (defined as children's paid or unpaid work done outside the family, frequently under exploitative conditions). Schildkrout (1981) explains that working inside the family structure differs from working for wages in the labor market, because the child outgrows the dependency relationship with the family in the first case, but remains a wage earner in the second case: "A child worker, working for wages in a wage economy, is a worker who happens to be a child. A child who works in a familial context is a child who happens to work" (p. 101). Clearly, child work is characteristic of preindustrial, traditional societies and plays an important part in socialization for adult roles, particularly sex roles. Child labor, in contrast, although based on traditional social attitudes about the role of children, evolves under conditions of poverty caused by industrialization and by exploitation-based changes in modes of production. This phenomenon was particularly evident in the West both during the nineteenth century and during the early part of the twentieth century. Nevertheless, additional industrialization and development in the West, fueled largely by colonialism, helped the West to outgrow its need for child labor. Instead, there was a growing need in industry for trained and educated adults, a need that could be met only through establishing our modern public school system (see Osterman, 1979).

The process of evolution from preindustrial to industrial modes of production has been quite distinct in Third World countries. Because of their inferior positions within the world economy, developing countries have enjoyed only limited success in industrializing their economies. Development has been uneven, occurring in the modern sector at a rapid pace while the rural sector simultaneously has become more impoverished. Aside from natural resources, these countries' exports have often been in the labor-intensive agricultural goods or artisanal industries. Given the high rate of unemployment and poverty in the Third World, inexpensive child labor seems understandable as a consequence.

Documentary evidence from a number of Third World countries suggests that the transformation of child work into child labor has not been a lengthy process; rather, it has been brutally short, occurring over the course of only two or three generations, causing dislocation and atomization of families. The phenomenon of child labor is as symptomatic of the Third World's underdevelopment as malnutrition or disease are in many Third World countries. While it is beyond the scope of this chapter to consider any of these case issues in greater detail, the following bibliography may encourage more research attention to the problems of child labor.

Annotated Bibliography

Aghajamian, A. "Family Economy and Economic Contribution of Children in Iran: An Overview." *Journal of South Asian and Middle Eastern Studies,* 1979, *3,* 21–30.

This is a discussion of the direct labor contribution of children in Iran prior to the shah's overthrow, where the minimum work age until recently was ten years. It examines social, economic, and sex differences affecting work participation. The author singles out as significant the positive relationship between land availability and boys in child work, as well as the negative relationship between the availability of agricultural machinery and work for boys.

Anti-Slavery Society for the Protection of Human Rights. *Child Labour in Morocco's Carpet Industry.* London: Russell Press, 1978.

This is a study of child labor in a vital sector of the Moroccan economy—the carpet industry, comprising 59 percent of all craft exports. The author explains how government policies, geared to increasing industrialization, indirectly have fostered an increase in child labor. While underplaying the importance of child labor, the government actually has encouraged it by subsidizing the carpet industry, which has made Morocco the number-one producer of carpets for export. At the same time, carpet making has changed from a craft to a cottage industry, with a consequent effect on the composition of the labor force. Today the owner contracts for labor through a *maalema*, paid by the square meter, who hires a work force at the lowest possible cost. Morocco's burgeoning population (particularly school-age children in a country with inadequate educational facilities) guarantees a labor surplus of children, especially young girls sent to work by their parents. This report is particularly useful for its discussion of the role of governments and industry in perpetuating the problem of child labor.

Banarjee, S. *Child Labour in India.* London: Anti-Slavery Society, 1979.

The author summarizes the historical background of child labor in India, along with its contemporary manifestations. The book gives a statistical and descriptive survey and examines the economic and social dimensions of child employment, particularly its depressant effects on adult wages and on education. It then describes child labor in the brick kiln industry and the *zari* embroidery industry. The author points out that, although legislation exists forbidding child labor, the laws are universally ignored for economic and social reasons; therefore, change cannot be brought about by legal fiat, as it would have disastrous consequences. The author advocates instead a series of short-term measures to improve the lot of working children by regulating work conditions and encouraging educational, medical, and recreational facilities.

Bekombo, M. "The Child in Africa: Socialisation, Education, and Work." In G. Rodgers and G. Standing (Eds.), *Child Work, Poverty, and Underdevelopment.* Geneva: International Labour Organization, 1981.

This article places child labor within the socioeconomic structure of African society. Two important issues are raised. First, the socialization of children in traditional African society is greatly dependent upon children's participation in domestic activities, both within the nuclear family and in the extended kinship structure. Children's integration through work is thus closer in function to education than it is to paid work. Second, urbanization has altered this fundamental process because children's work is much less dependent on kinship ties than on wage relationships; thus, the way is open to greater exploitation. The traditional family structure has been eroded, with consequences for parental authority and children's frame of reference. This article is extremely useful for its description of the African education and socialization systems.

Bromley, R. "Organization, Regulation, and Exploitation in the So-Called Urban Informal Sector: The Street-Traders of Cali, Colombia." *World Development*, 1978, 6, 1160-1171.

This is an interesting discussion of the urban informal sector — its structure, its organization, and its relationship to both the formal sector and the government. At least 10 percent of the total numbers of workers in Colombia are underage street traders (under fourteen — sellers of contaminated food or street newspaper vendors hired illegally by middlemen for newspaper companies to avoid paying benefits and minimum wages). The author criticizes the International Labor Organization (ILO) interpretation of the urban informal sector. The official ILO view emphasizes small, labor-intensive businesses within a strategy of development because they are entrepreneurial and independent of authorities and of big business. According to the author's interpretation, this view ignores linkages with the formal sector, as well as the fact that many street traders are little more than disenfranchised employees of larger enterprises (p. 1168). The street traders, locked as they are into poverty, economic insecurity, and continuing debt to the formal sector, are rarely able to accumulate capital and formalize their businesses in the way envisaged by the ILO.

Cain, M. "The Economic Activities of Children in a Village in Bangladesh." *Population and Development Review*, 1977, 5, 405-438.

This article analyzes the fertility decisions made by households, as well as the relationships of these decisions to a child's productivity in contributing to the household's economic welfare. Demand for household labor is divided along sex lines into labor needed for household maintenance and upkeep and labor generating income and capital. The interrelated factors affecting the rate of increase in a child's productivity depend on the beginning work age, the child's time input into work, and child's productivity and labor efficiency relative to an adult, and the child's net productivity. The author concludes that, because of the economic impact of child labor, both high fertility and large numbers of children are "economically rational propositions." Male children in particular become net producers by age twelve, compensate for their consumption by age fifteen, and can compensate both for their own and for one sister's consumption by age twenty-two.

Cain, M., and Khorshed, A. B. M. "Labour Market Structure and Reproductive Behavior in Rural South Asia." In G. Rodgers and G. Standing (Eds.), *Child Work, Poverty, and Underdevelopment.* Geneva: International Labour Organization, 1981.

This article holds that the relationship between the economic value of children and fertility must be understood within the larger context of the labor market structure. The labor market can increase or decrease parental need for children's labor to such an extent that "the same net return for child labour may have an entirely different significance for reproductive behavior, depending on the setting" (p. 245). The authors review various theories of labor market structure and illustrate how structure can influence child labor. They conclude by discussing implications of the analysis of child labor, market structure, and fertility in rural Bangladesh. The authors make two additional points: First, there is a floor to real wage rates, but there is continuing downward pressure on those rates, which postpones the elimination of child labour as a paying proposition for parents. Second, sex-segregated markets affect fertility both by constraining female children's productivity and by imposing additional economic dependence on women.

Chan, P. "The Forgotten Little People." *Asian Economies,* 1975, *15,* 67-79.

This article examines child labor in Kuala Lumpur, Malaysia. It is primarily a survey of the social and economic background of the child and the family, work conditions, wages and other incomes, expenses and savings patterns, and the child's attitude toward work and the future. According to the author, child work is a function both of supply and of demand factors. The supply factors include urban poverty, unemployment, and absence of compulsory education, while demand factors include the existence of job opportunities—and of employers willing to hire children—in both the formal and the informal sectors. Another important factor is government neglect and reluctance to enforce existing legislation. The adverse consequences of child work include high social-opportunity costs and a continuance of the cycle of poverty.

Costin, L. "School and Employment: Protection and Opportunity." In L. Costin (Ed.), *Child Welfare: Policies and Practice.* New York: McGraw Hill, 1972.

This is a historical survey of (1) child labor in America at the turn of this century and (2) the development of the public education movement. It examines a variety of beliefs that have influenced public opinion and created changes in labor legislation. Initially, society held that parents had a duty to train their children for work and had the right to send them to work; now, this viewpoint has changed to the attitude that children have a right to education and to protection from exploitation. Each of these public attitudes has had an impact on relevant legislation aimed at controlling child employment and providing educational opportunities.

Dalela, S. C. "No Time to Play or Dream." *Social Welfare,* 1976, *23,* 8-9.

This article is part of a special issue of *Social Welfare* devoted to child labor. The article suggests that poverty and illiteracy are the main causes of child labor, but acknowledges that it would be unfeasible to eradicate it in the near future. Therefore, according to the author, it is more realistic to accept it as an unavoidable evil while working to provide education and better conditions for child laborers.

Daniel, J. C. "Child Worker Has Come to Stay?" *Social Welfare,* 1976, *23,* 6-7.

This is another treatment of child labor in India, emphasizing its growth and the ineffectiveness of existing legislation. The author offers a number of suggestions to improve the condition of working children. He stresses, among other points, that the Indian educational system is inadequate for the psychological, economic, and social needs of children because it is irrelevant to earning a living. Curricula should be revamped to make them more meaningful to children's needs and interests. Alternative programs teaching crafts and industrial skills could be established to help potential dropouts earn money and obtain work experience.

Davies, E. "Work Out of School." *Education,* November 1972, *140* (19), 1-4.

This article deals exclusively with part-time employment of English schoolchildren between the ages of thirteen and fifteen. It examines the effectiveness of existing legislation and connections between part-time employment and factors contributing to educational development. Types of employment included summer jobs, pre- and postschool work, babysitting, and family assistance. The author concludes that there is a negative relationship between heavy involvement in part-time work and poorer attitudes toward school and school work.

De la Luz Silva, M. "Urban Policy and Child Work: Elements for the Analysis of Child Work in Chile." In G. Rodgers and G. Standing (Eds.), *Child Work, Poverty, and Underdevelopment.* Geneva: International Labour Organization, 1981.

This article defines the changing role of children in relationship to unemployment in Chile. It investigates the economic causes of child labor, classifies the economic activities of children, and reviews the effects work has on children. The author provides a useful definition of work—"any socially useful, remunerable activity requiring manual and/or intellectual effort and conscious, purposeful action; that is, the production of a good or performance of a service" (p. 166).

Dube, L. "The Economic Roles of Children in India: Methodological Issues." In G. Rodgers and G. Standing (Eds.), *Child Work, Poverty, and Underdevelopment.* Geneva: International Labour Organization, 1981.

This is a study of the economic role of children in India. It is useful for its analysis of children and work within the Indian and Hindu cultural traditions. The author argues that throughout India—in rural areas, tribal groups, and urban areas—children's participation in work is entirely within the indigenous cultural tradition, because work has been an important socializing device.

Easy, W. "Notes on Child Labour in Hong Kong." *Race and Class,* 1977, 22, 377-381.

This is a study comparing child labor in contemporary Hong Kong with its historical antecedent in nineteenth-century Britain. While both are typical of the early stages of industrialization, the factors that ended child work in Britain are not present in Hong Kong, making child labor more difficult to eradicate. Hong Kong is an enclave economy with no natural resources of its own except a large population. It relies on light industrial manufacturing geared toward export. Entrepreneurs are given free rein in the economy, with little government interference. At the same time the labor unions, weak and divided, are prevented by legislation from organizing for collective bargaining or to obtain social security. As a result, labor costs are extremely low, making it easier for industrialists to exploit sudden fads in the world market. As a surplus work force, children are extensively employed to drive wages even lower. Their exploitation is tolerated by all parties concerned, including families. This study's comparison of Hong Kong with Western Europe is particularly useful.

Engle, P. L., and Butz, W. P. "Methodological Issues in Collecting Time-Use Data in Developing Countries." Paper presented at the symposium of the Society for Research in Child Development, Boston, April 1981.

This is an excellent article, which analyzes the methodology used by anthropologists and economists in documenting people's time use in nonindustrialized countries. Time-use studies are employed to calculate opportunity cost of women's time spent at home, to estimate work in the informal sector, and to analyze the pattern of agricultural productivity. The article very usefully summarizes unpublished research on the time use of women and children. In particular, it questions the validity of studies that rely solely on parents' reports of their children's activities, since parents tend to underestimate their children's contributions.

Gopolan, M., and Kulandaiswamy, V. "Child Labour." *Social Welfare*, 1976, *23*, 1-3.

In this survey of the prevalence of child labor in the Indian economy, one interesting point raised is that fact that the Harijan, or untouchable, caste appears to contribute the greatest proportion of child workers to the labor force. The author makes a number of suggestions to alleviate the problem, including better enforcement of existing legislation, research into the extent of child employment, and vocationalization of education.

Hamilton, C. "Increased Child Labour: An External Diseconomy of Rural Employment Creation for Adults." *Asian Economies*, 1980, *35*, 30-39.

This article analyzes data from India and Egypt, two examples of excess labour economies. It suggests that programs to increase adult rural employment have the ultimate effect increasing child labor, a fact to be taken into consideration by rural planners. This phenomenon occurs because women and children are used for farm labor, which permits men to take jobs outside the family farm. One important aspect of child labor examined by this author is the connection between child labor and primary education; there are additional unforeseen costs of child labor. *Functional literacy* is usually defined as "such an ability to read that it will not fall back into illiteracy after having left school" (p. 38) and is allegedly attained after three to five years at school. But most children have to work to such an extent that they never reach functional literacy; therefore, resources spent on their education are essentially wasted. These resources include government funds as well as children's income forgone by families. Thus, extension of primary education to rural areas may inadvertently lead to greater educational inequality, since only comparatively well-off families can afford to keep their children in school.

Heywood, C. "The Market for Children in Nineteenth-Century France." *History*, 1981, *66*, 34-49.

This is an interesting article, which documents change in children's economic roles as a consequence of the Industrial Revolution, by means of a study of supply and demand of the wage force. It challenges the dual notions that child labor increased drastically during the nineteenth century and thus led to a change in public opinion, which in turn brought about the eventual abolition of child labor and the expansion of public education. The author asserts that along with women, children were already widely employed in the textile and spinning industries, and there was a decrease in children's rate of participation following initial intensification at the beginning of the century. Citing primary-source evidence, he proposes that child labor was abolished for economic reasons, not for political or humanitarian ones. He also suggests that employers did not hire children on the basis of their cheapness, their physical advantages, and their docility: Both relatively and absolutely, children are less economically productive than adults, which explains why employers were willing to stop hiring children, even without the pressure of legislation.

Hull, T. "Perspectives and Data Requirements for the Study of Children's Work." In G. Rodgers and G. Standing (Eds.), *Child Work, Labor, and Underdevelopment.* Geneva: International Labour Organization, 1981.

This is an important article examining the prevailing paradigms and orientations of child-labor research that affect understanding of this issue. One interesting suggestion is that the prevailing paradigms in Western studies of child labor are shaped by nineteenth-century normative attitudes. The original reform movement that led to the abolition of child labor in the factories was strengthened by the growth of scientific methods. Western studies took the normative approach that child employment was inherently bad and then set out to prove this notion through the use of data collection and objective reasoning. At the same time, rural anthropologists in colonial outposts were developing such concepts as socialization and suggesting that one way children acquired cultural characteristics and behavior was through work undertaken in childhood and adolescence. This article also provides an excellent introduction to the methodology of child-labor research.

International Labor Organization. *Report of the ILO/SIDA Asian Regional Seminar on Labor Inspection to the Employment of Women and Protection of Children.* Geneva: International Labour Organization, 1973.

This document is the result of a seminar on labor inspection in Asia. Although some of the material is somewhat dated, it is useful for its review of the national and international labor legislation for women and children in Asia. Specific points of discussion include employment opportunities for women; the scope of labor legislation coverage relating to women and children and gaps perceived by inspectors; the organization and methods of labor inspection, including practical difficulties for carrying out visits; occupational health and safety; and training for labor inspectors. In general, labor inspectors have been criticized in the literature dealing with child employment; this report helps document many of their problems and frustrations.

International Textile, Garment, and Leather Workers Federation. *Employment of Children and Young People: Textile, Garment, and Leather Sectors.* Amsterdam: First World Congress, 1972.

This report is based on replies from affiliates of the union. It reports on minimum-age legislation, wage levels, and legislation of work conditions in a total of twenty-four countries. A comparison is made between developed countries, where conditions are considered good, and developing countries such as India and Hong Kong. This report is difficult to interpret, because it treats national union reports uncritically.

Iyer, K. V. "Role of Children in the Indian Economy." *Social Welfare,* 1968, *15,* 1-3.

    This article discusses the role of children in the Indian economy, the sectors that employ them, legislative and welfare measures for their protection, and educational facilities available to them in light of India's current population explosion and the ever growing proportion of children. Although somewhat dated, this article provides a helpful representation of the different sectors that employ children, particularly agriculture and village or cottage industries. The worst conditions prevail in this last sector because it is not covered by legislation concerning work hours, conditions, wages, or minimum age. It is difficult even to estimate the extent of employment in cottage industries, as most employment is obtained indirectly through parents or other mediators.

Kitteringham, J. "Country Girls in Nineteenth-Century England." In R. Samuel (Ed.), *Village Life and Labour.* London: Routledge & Kegan Paul, 1975.

    This article considers the role of the country working girl in nineteenth-century England. The author uses primary-source material to document the many and varied tasks of girls in farming, domestic service, crafts, and industry. She describes, among other practices, the use of agricultural gangs—primarily young girls working in the fields and following the harvests from farm to farm. A middle-class movement in the 1860s set out to abolish farm gangs and educate the children of the working class, because the prevailing Victorian value system of the day condemned work for girls and children as conducive to immorality. Compulsory education began with the Education Act of 1870, and agricultural gangs of children who were under ten years old were made illegal in 1875. The article states, however, that girls were not removed from work until the mechanization of agriculture, since local authorities were loath to enforce compulsory education at public expense. This article offers many useful points of comparison with the phenomenon of child labor in the Third World.

Knight, W. J. *The World's Exploited Children Growing up Sadly.* U.S. Department of Labor Bureau of International Affairs monograph no. 4. Washington, D.C.: U.S. Government Printing Office, 1980.

    This is a general overview of the problem of child labor. It examines both national and international legislation and includes an appendix with various resolutions and recommendations. It offers relatively unsystematic statistics and descriptions of child labor in a number of countries. No supporting footnotes or bibliography are supplied.

Kuchero, T. "Exploitation of Children Widespread." *Monthly Labor Review* (ILO Reports), 1980, *105,* 43–45.

    This is a short factual summary of the ILO report *Children at Work* by Mendelievich. It deals both with statistics and with examples of child labor in many different occupations throughout the world. It also treats the physical, social, economic, and educational consequences of child work.

Landes, W., and Solmon, L. C. "Compulsory Schooling Legislation: An Economic Analysis of Law and Social Change in the Nineteenth Century." *The Journal of Economic History,* 1972, *33,* 45–84.

    This is a technical discussion of the effect that compulsory school legislation had on school attendance in the United States in the late nineteenth century. By examining census data and school enrollment and attendance figures, the authors conclude that the passage of such legislation in the 1870s did not cause the reported increase in school attendance; rather, the authors maintain that high levels of schooling preceding passage of the legislation and were in part responsible for these laws. Contrary to their expectations, the authors did not find that either the presence or the absence of child labor laws had a significant impact on school attendance, although they suggest that a more thorough analysis of child-labor laws, children's labor-force behavior, and the effects of other legislation might be made.

Marla, S. "Bonded Labour in the Mendak District (AP)." *A National Labour Institute Bulletin,* Bombay, n.d., 424–430.

    This is an interesting description of the phenomenon of bonded labor in India, under which a child or an adult is leased to a master by a parent or other relative. He or she, like the bonded servants of colonial America, serves that master as a virtual slave for a set period of time. In most cases, the individual is bonded during childhood in exchange for a loan or to pay for a wedding or a funeral. The individual can be bonded again at the end of the initial period. The landless classes often are obliged to sell their children into bondage in order to eat.

Mendelievich, E. "Child Labour." *International Labour Review,* 1979a, *118,* 557–569.

    This is a factual report of ILO activities concerning working children. The author provides statistics on child labor along with a survey of existing national and international legislation, and he examines the causes of child labor both in developed and in developing countries. He also describes some of the economic, social, physical, and psychological consequences of child employment both for the individual and for society. The author concludes that real reform will not occur until there is a change in budgetary priorities, with greater emphasis given to human development and redistribution of income.

Mendelievich, E. *Children at Work.* Geneva: International Labour Organization, 1979b.

This volume consists of a long introductory essay and ten case studies of child labor in the world. The introduction is a well-organized and systematic exposition of every aspect of child labor. Countries studied include Argentina, Greece, India, Italy, Mexico, Nigeria, Pakistan, Peru, and Thailand.

Mendelievich, E. "Forgotten Army of Child Workers." *UNESCO Courier,* 1980, 19–24.

This article summarizes how exploitative child labor occurred in the West in the early stages of the Industrial Revolution, when neither institutions nor legislation were adequate for the new circumstances. The gradual abolition of child labor, however, was inspired more by the desire to increase adult employment than by humanitarian motivations. This fact is important because similar circumstances of industrialization exist in developing countries today and have fostered a phenomenal increase in child labor. Rapid urbanization and dislocation from traditional life-styles are directly associated with increased adult unemployment and with greater use of children's labor.

Minge-Kalman, W. "The Industrial Revolution and the European Family: The Institutionalization of 'Childhood' as a Market for Family Labour." *Comparative Studies in Society and History,* 1978, *20,* 454–468.

This article analyzes the impact of the Industrial Revolution on the family in Western society. The author suggests that the Industrial Revolution displaced the family as an economic producer of goods, but also gave it a new role as reproducer of educated labor necessary to production. The development of the institution of childhood extended children's dependency into adolescence, turning children into a "labor-intensive, capital-intensive product of the family."

Mitchell, D., and Clapp, J. "The Impact of Child Labor Laws on Kinds of Jobs Held by Young School-Leavers." *Journal of Human Resources,* 1980, *15,* 396–408.

This article analyzes the impact of the Fair Labor Standards Act of 1938, which regulates the employment of American teenagers fourteen through seventeen years old. It uses census data to identify shifting employment in sectors of the economy not covered by the law. In its historical survey of legislation, the article notes how state child-labor laws interacted with school-leaving laws and workmen's compensation laws. This article provides an interesting historical background on child labor in America.

Morice, A. "The Exploitation of Children in the 'Informal Sector': Proposals for Research." In G. Rodgers and G. Standing (Eds.), *Child Work, Poverty, and Underdevelopment.* Geneva: International Labour Organization, 1981.

This essay identifies obstacles to research on child labor in the informal sectors of developing countries and suggests that better qualitative and anthropological research methods be adopted. The author also provides a useful discussion of interest groups that have avoided the investigation of child labor, governments, international organizations, employers, families, and the children themselves.

Mueller, E. "The Economic Value of Children in Peasant Agriculture." In R. Ridker (Ed.), *Population and Development.* Baltimore: Johns Hopkins University Press, 1976.

This article analyzes the value of children in peasant agriculture to determine how much males and females contribute, respectively, to household economies. The author considers the economic role of children compared to that of adults and the aged and concludes that, in aggregate models of consumption and production, children have a negative net worth in peasant societies, but "from the viewpoint of the individual couple, a large family may offer economic benefits at certain stages of the life cycle" (p. 103).

Nag, M., Peet, R. C., and White, B. "Economic Value of Children in Two Peasant Societies." *International Population Conference (Mexico, 1977).* Vol. 1. Liege: International Union for the Scientific Study of Population, 1978.

This article is a study of the economic value of children in the peasant societies of Java and Nepal and examines economic interpretations of fertility. It estimates the average amount of time spent by children in various activities and the extent to which these activities contribute to parents' welfare. Issues discussed include age differences, sex differences, differences in family size, household economic efficiency, and the value of children as old-age security. Among other findings, the authors discovered that girls twelve to fourteen years old work almost as much as boys over fifteen, while girls fifteen to nineteen years old work more than boys over fifteen. The article also challenges the belief that children in peasant cultures have limited or negative economic value. It appears that the work input of children under fifteen is quite substantial, giving children a significant positive economic value in addition to their value as old-age security for their parents.

Nagi, M. "Child Labour in Rural Egypt." *Rural Sociology,* 1972, *37,* 623-625.

This brief article analyzes the presence of extensive child employment in Egypt. Child labor is so institutionalized that the Egyptian census uses the ages of five and six years as the lowest cutoffs to define the labor force. There are sex differences in child labor, with more girls working now relative to the entire child population than ever before. The author suggests that this increase reflects both the better adaptability of young girls to domestic work and the cultural biases of families which send girls to work in order to pay for boys' educations.

Osterman, P. "Education and Labor Markets at the Turn of the Century." *Politics and Society,* 1979, *9,* 103-122.

This article explores the nature of the relationship between two forces that shaped modern American society at the turn of the century. The first was the revolution in productive and distributive capabilities along with the growth of conglomerates. The second was the growth of the institution (and bureaucratic structure) of our modern public school system. During this period at the turn of the century, economic reliance on child labor decreased because the changing technology required an adult work force, which was provided by the rising tide of East and South European immigrants. As a consequence, employers were less resistant to reformers seeking to abolish child labor and increase the length of compulsory schooling. "The impetus for this reform came in part from the well-meant feelings of people disturbed by the exploitative essence of child labor, but it also came from the need of the middle class to find new forms of social control and of economic access into emerging white-collar jobs" (p. 103).

Porter, R. "Child Labour in Hong Kong and Related Problems: A Brief Review." *International Labour Review,* 1975, *114,* 427-440.

This article suggests that child labor in Hong Kong is the result of government unwillingness or inability to enforce existing legislation, which dates back to 1922. Also, child labor is very prevalent, not only for the obvious economic reason of low wages but also because primary education is not compulsory and secondary education is restricted and expensive. The author proposes that cash allowances be given to those poor families who send their children to school rather than to work.

Premi, M. "Student Workers in the Age Group Five-Fourteen: A Socio-Demographic Analysis." *Manpower Journal,* 1973, *18,* 68-84.

A dated but somewhat useful analysis of child labor in India, using 1961 census data to examine the proportion of child workers, both male and female, in the rural and urban sectors of various states. The author notes that the 1971 census changed its categories of workers, thereby giving a truer picture of part-time workers (that is, students who work and attend school).

Repetto, R. G. "Direct Economic Costs and Value of Children." In R. C. Ridker (Ed.), *Population and Development.* Baltimore: Johns Hopkins University Press, 1976.

This article is a study of effects that changes in the economic costs and value of children have had on fertility decisions. The study's purpose is to assist in the development of government policies capable of manipulating these effects. It considers the value of children's earnings as well as nonmarket household labor and later parental support. Costs involved include only the value of the child's consumption and exclude the lost-opportunity cost of the mother's time in child care.

Rodgers, G., and Standing, G. *Child Work, Poverty, and Underdevelopment.* Geneva: International Labour Organization, 1981a.

This is an important collection of essays on child labor, dealing with methodological issues (Hull, Morice); economic interpretations (Rosenzweig, Cain, and Mozumder); and case studies on Chile, India, Nigeria, and Africa (De la Luz Silva, Dube, Schildkrout, Bekombo). The introduction by Rodgers and Standing integrates these essays into a comprehensive analytical framework and raises important points concerning the relationship between the prevalent mode of production in society and the types of activity a child engages in.

Rodgers, G., and Standing, G. "Economic Roles of Children in Low-Income Countries." *International Labor Review,* 1981b, *120* (1), 31-47.

The authors contend that work is not a child's main activity in most societies. Instead, they describe a system for classifying children's activities according to the nature of the activity and the amount of time spent. They then apply this system to describe child work in the Third World. This article is possibly the best existing short treatment of the subject matter.

Rosenzweig, M. R. "Household and Nonhousehold Activities of Youths: Issues of Modelling, Data, and Estimation Strategies." In G. Rodgers, and G. Standing (Eds.), *Child Work, Poverty, and Underdevelopment.* Geneva: International Labour Organization, 1981.

This is an econometric analysis of children's roles and children's contributions to household economy. It considers several alternative household models and then tests these models with microsurvey data. It deals with the interrelationship between the employment of adult women and (1) the labor force participation and (2) schooling of both male and female children. According to this study, there is evidence that an increase in adult female employment and wage rate leads to greater household labor for girls and less participation in school for boys. In contrast, an increase in the male wage rate seems to increase children's school attendance rates for both sexes.

Schildkrout, E. "The Employment of Children in Kano (Nigeria)." In G. Rodgers and G. Standing (Eds.), *Child Work, Poverty, and Underdevelopment.* Geneva: International Labour Organization, 1981.

This article considers the relationship between roles and activities of children (including school attendance) and socioeconomic status of parents. One important finding concerns the importance of intervening cultural factors in determining children's roles. In Nigeria, the Muslim institution of *purdah* could not function if it were not for the presence of children to help women carry out domestic tasks. Recent government attempts to expand public education have prevented children from fulfilling this role and will thus have a profound effect not only on future generations of women but also on the institution of *purdah* itself.

Sengupta, P. "Children Work to Live." *Social Welfare,* 1975, *22,* 11-12.

This article makes useful points concerning the future of children who are forced to work at early ages. The author notes that child labor is condemned more often as a social evil than as an economic practice, but points out that the nature of work, working conditions, potential dangers, and the obstacles to children's development should all be considered in assessing whether child labor is an evil practice or an economic necessity.

Stern, D., Smith, S., and Doolittle, F. "How Children Used to Work." *Law and Contemporary Problems,* 1975, *39,* 93-117.

This article discusses how the changing mode of economic production in the United States over the last 150 years has changed the economic role of children. It specifically deals with "the increasing conflict between child rearing and other activities of the parents, the curtailment of child labor, and the decreased importance of children to parents as a source of old-age financial support" (p. 93). It also discusses the relationship of this trend to the historical decline in fertility and concludes with an examination of the advantages and disadvantages of excluding children from the labor force.

Tienda, M. "Economic Activity of Children in Peru's Labour Force: Behavior in Rural and Urban Contexts." *Rural Sociology,* 1979, *44,* 370-391.

This article is an analysis both of the economic value of children in Peru and of the way in which changes in production deriving from economic growth and development have influenced the organization of the household economy and changed the value of children to their parents. By studying the socioeconomic, demographic, and familial forces that influence children's propensity to work, it examines children's work in rural and urban areas. The author concludes that rural children are more than twice as likely to be economically active than urban children. Also, sex differences in labor force participation occur at an early age and gradually widen.

Vlassoff, M. "Labour Demand and Economic Utility of Children: A Case Study of Rural India." *Population Studies,* 1979, *33,* 415-428.

This article is an analysis of the economic utility of children. It considers the cost of children in an agricultural setting, the timing of fertility, and the relative level of rural unemployment. The significance of the child's contribution to the household economy is studied along with the quantity and the quality of work provided, the links of that work to poverty versus relative labor scarcity, and the extent to which adult men perceive children as economically useful. The author claims that, in the village studied, the economic costs of children far outweigh the benefits. He found that young children do not make significant economic contributions, either in their own judgment or in that of their fathers. In contrast to other researchers in this area, the author found that there was no difference in the economic utility of children according to socioeconomic status.

Weisner, T., and Gallimore, R. "My Brother's Keeper: Child and Sibling Caretaking." *Current Anthropology,* 1977, *18* (2), 169-190.

This article considers the little-studied but widespread phenomenon of child and sibling caretaking. It points out that most theories of socialization, because they are Western-derived, ignore caretaking by anyone other than the mother. It concludes that sibling caretaking may contribute an additional and important class of variables to fine-grained analyses of sibling-sibling influence and status. It also suggests that, because children perform their caretaking roles differently from parents, there may be unanticipated effects, both on the caretakers and on their charges.

Zamir, I. "The Market of Children at Erez Junction." *MERIP,* 1979, *9,* 23-24.

This is a journalistic account of a market where children appear on a daily basis to have their labor auctioned of by *ra'is* (Arab bosses). The children are sent to work by their families and are dispatched to settlements to pick fruit, vegetables, and flowers.

References

Aries, P. *Centuries of Childhood.* New York: Random House, 1962.
Beuf, A., and Kurz, D. (Eds.) *Childhood: A Social Construct.* Lexington, Mass.: Ginn, 1980.
De Mause, L. (Ed.) *The History of Childhood.* New York: Psychohistory Press, 1974.
Plumb, J. H. "The Great Change in Children." In A. Beuf and D. Kurz (Eds.), *Childhood: A Social Construct.* Lexington, Mass.: Ginn, 1980.
Ridker, R. C. (Ed.). *Population and Development.* Baltimore: Johns Hopkins University Press, 1976.

Elizabeth B. Moore is in the doctoral program in international relations at the University of Pennsylvania. She has worked previously with the Food and Agriculture Organization in Rome and has recently been doing fieldwork in North Africa as part of the Morocco Literacy Project.

A long-time observer of international development provides a foundation perspective on the potential of applied research for children in the developing world.

What Policy Relevance Can Mean

Francis X. Sutton

It has been an aspiration of this session on child development and international development to display a range of investigations that may guide the development policies of governments, international agencies, and others. The relevance of these various investigations evidently depends on what policies are, and I hope it may be useful to begin by recalling something of the diversity of what passes for policy.

Any deliberate program of public action poses a great array of questions about effective organization, combinations of resources, and expected costs and benefits. Such a program must be planned, monitored, revised as things go along, assessed with more or less rigor and formality at various stages, and perhaps brought to an end (if, indeed, it ever consciously is). At every stage in the process, there is typically recourse to generally accepted principles, common sense, the accumulated expertise of bureaucrats, and information and analysis from others, possibly including professional social scientists. The process of rationalization that so intrigued Max Weber has been going on for a long time and has in the last decade brought increasing

This chapter is a discussion of papers presented at a session on child development and international development, which was part of the meetings of the American Association for the Advancement of Science held in Washington, D.C., on January 4, 1982. (The same papers appear in the sourcebook as Chapters One, Two, Three, Four, and Five.)

D. A. Wagner (Ed.). *Child Development and International Development: Research-Policy Interfaces.*
New Directions for Child Development, no. 20. San Francisco: Jossey-Bass, June 1983. **107**

recourse to the buttressing of bureaucratic powers with the research of professional social scientists. Great opportunities have opened up for applied research within the framework of action programs; and, indeed, in some subjects such research makes up the bulk of what is done. Applied research of this sort is only sparsely represented in what we have heard during this session, and I should remind you of this unrepresentativeness of our sampling. For example, studies like Wagner's are not, in my experience, typical of the research on literacy. We had occasion three or four years ago to devote the annual meeting of the Bellagio "Indians" (who serve the "chiefs" of international agencies engaged in education in developing countries) to literacy programs. On that occasion, only one of the papers escaped from the operational problems of the literacy campaigns that have been launched in the last decades.

But not all the work that passes as policy-relevant is in the service of deliberate programs, their operational design, and their evaluation. Governments, international agencies, and others always have very broad aspirations or principles that they are attempting to serve or justify. They need arguments and evidence that they are on the right track, aiming at some feasible goal, and perhaps making progress toward it. Sometimes they are even seeking basically new ideas. We are now very conscious that the dominant "public agenda" changes over time in ways that are not obviously dictated by the urgency or centrality of the topics in this agenda. After several decades of preoccupation with development and developing countries, we have seen the splendidly vague idea of development undergo great changes. The initial focus on the acquisition of sovereign independence by formerly colonial territories brought an emphasis on nation building and collective national economic progress. Only lately has emphasis shifted to equity, distribution, and the basic needs of the most disadvantaged. The papers presented in this symposium show quite clearly that our authors are keeping step with currently dominant concerns in the international public agenda of development. Child survival, effects of the employment of women on child care, provision for abandoned children, and the impact of the education of women on fertility and on mortality are all subjects more prominent now in the agenda of development than they were a few years ago. Investigations on these topics now have a fresh and heightened policy relevance. Some investigations—notably those showing the striking evidence of the effects of maternal education on child survival—have produced much excitement in development agencies. Cochrane and Mehra find an almost boring uniformity in the results on this matter across the developing countries; would that we could find such comforting boredom more often! In contrast, the evidence in Engle's paper that children in Guatemalan villages survive better with working mothers runs against received wisdom and will enrich the thin factual base for policy debates on this relationship.

But I would also ask you to note the absence from these papers of subjects like training for productivity, or national solidarity, or means of identifying and developing special talents. These are subjects still important to developing countries, and some years ago they were in the focus of policy attention, but nowadays have yielded to other concerns. Policy relevance thus means, in a certain sense, the following of fashion. I do not mean to suggest that such following is ignoble, but only to remind us that being relevant at any given time requires studying what is on the current public agenda, perhaps to the neglect of other important matters.

Research of the types reported in this symposium relate more to what the French call *finalités* than to concrete programs and policies that competent agencies can follow. To hear that the education of girls has the potential effects on child mortality that shine through the professional caution of Cochrane's and Nehra's paper, or which LeVine depicts for fertility in his, certainly encourages commitment to the education of girls. But this is a very broad indication for policy and one that is not easy for governments or others to follow. The sense of discouragement or despair that now hangs over educational policy in the developing countries — and is wishfully talked about as a transient crisis — is one of the sadder features of the present scene. While its roots are too spreading and entangled for me to trace here, neglect is certainly not one of them. Economists have long been troubled by the fraction of national budgets that education typically absorbs, and national governments are frustrated at the impossibility of meeting public demands that they cannot in good conscience resist. To have strong arguments for educating girls usefully counters dispositions to discriminate against girls, but it does not ease the problems of ministries of education already engulfed by needs and demands.

In these papers, there is much heartening evidence of beneficial effects of mass education that commonly have been either unperceived or lost amid doubts. The expansion of formal schooling in the developing countries has been fueled by popular perception of its relevance to economic opportunity. People have learned that education may lead to jobs. The Edwards and Todaro (1974) description of the demand for education as a "derived" demand for paid employment is one that I have always found realistic and persuasive, but the effects of this demand for education go far beyond the motivations that brought it, as this symposium illustrates. Work of the sort presented in this symposium provides encouraging evidence that the culturally alien character of Western-model schools is not all loss and that the changes it brings help societies cope with other changes that modernization brings. The poor quality of present schooling in many and perhaps most parts of the developing world is a cause of much lament, but the effects of schooling evidently go far beyond the content of the curriculum, as LeVine argues and as Caldwell (1979, 1980) has argued in the series of very stimulating papers to which LeVine refers. Girls who have been to school seem to learn how to think in ways that affect their marital and maternal behavior. It is also clear that we know too little about these effects and their consequences. LeVine tells of his unrewarded search for research reports on these matters, and it seems astonishing that Caldwell could not find serious field studies on such matters as the distribution of food within households in developing countries.

A discovery that the education of girls improves chances of child survival leads some of the more dynamic types of development enthusiasts toward curriculum tinkering. This may be all right and incidentally may provide some employment for researchers on educational innovation, but there are also matters to be looked into that seem more fundamental and more consequential. Cochrane and Mehra's tables appear to show that the effects of maternal education on chances of child survival are somewhat more pronounced for Africa than for the other continents. This result is not surprising to anyone who has observed the special social distinction that school attendance has brought in African settings, and, hence, the presumption of new competencies that Caldwell has stressed in his explanation of Nigerian data. Of course, the displacement of old statuses and authority by the newly educated has been commonplace in the observation of African development over several decades, but one must ask how this elevation of the educated may be changing as education becomes more widespread and as the rewarding of the educated through wage employment becomes more uncertain and more frequently frustrated. As the experience of schooling becomes banal, part of everyone's life, may not some of its beneficial effects be diminished, too? A continuing study of the meaning and value of having been to school thus would seem to be a necessary part of the background for enlightened public policy — and likely to be of more use than curriculum tinkering.

Reflections of this sort bring us easily to the now familiar pleas for more field studies providing description and analysis, in the style beloved of anthropologists. I am sure such a view will not be displeasing in this setting, and it is now heard in enough places to make one think it an obviously necessary direction of effort. The paper by Mary Hollnsteiner and Peter Taçon reminds us that we are not referring only to studies in villages, but that the developing world is fast urbanizing and, whether people are already in the cities or only contemplating migration, their lives and expectations are affected by the lures and trials the cities offer. We know from various studies — for example, Joyce Moock's (1974) on Western Kenya — how schooling contributes to stimulating movement to the cities and to the swelling of the social pathologies Hollnsteiner and Taçon depict for us. The unmanageability of great urban agglomerations in the developing countries is now one of the more evident symptoms of the overburdening and impotence of governments. How people cope with gross inadequacies of economic opportunity and public services is a painful, necessary, and occasionally even inspiring subject for study, and the present disposition to seek out private initiatives and try to help "natural" social movements requires a base of information and analysis of this sort. There was, perhaps, a time when national plans provided a secure framework in which most of the agenda for policy-relevant research could be defined, but such is hardly the case any longer.

Wagner's paper addresses a somewhat different set of policy problems in developing countries and, seen in conjunction with the other papers, provokes reflections on the distinctions of literacy and Western-style schooling. One can with justification speak of a literacy imperative that is now a part of international morality. As Wagner points out, there can be reasonable doubts about decisive contributions of literacy to productivity and economic development, and the disruptive social effects schooling can have on "preliterate" societies have frequently been given worried notice. Nevertheless, the imperative remains as an axiom of public policy, and devising the means to generalize literacy without incurring crippling costs is a recurring challenge to governments. Indigenous systems of education have certainly been too little regarded, the prejudices against Islamic or Quranic education being familiar to anyone who has ever encountered this widespread form of teaching. The merits of indigenous educational systems that Wagner points out to us contrast with some of those we have been noticing in Western imports. Indigenous systems have cultural roots that the imports lack, but Wagner also shows us that movements toward kinds of educational syncretism with the modern imports promise a domestication of the modern school that has been demanded but too often left in windy rhetoric. Movements of this sort obviously pose difficult and sensitive issues for national governments and outsiders, but if it be accepted that such movements are necessary features of universalizing literacy and effecting its cultural domestication, then ignorance of them is perilous. I should also like to suggest that the kind of phenomenon Wagner describes seems not confined to Islam. The French geographer and urbanist Marc Pain has recently (1981) suggested that the only institutions keeping pace with the explosive growth of Kinshasa (Zaire) are the indigenous, and mostly Christian, religious organizations. It is through and around these religious groupings that the new migrants find at least some of the means of coping with their problems, and these groupings are certainly an important focus of nonformal education, which goes on without much external notice or assistance. We now look back on the early years of this era of our commitment to development as years of naive, youthful enthusiasm. Our simple faith that development could be planned, controlled, and rapid has withered amid troubles and futilities, but in the five papers in this symposium, we have seen that there is little justification for despair. The great social revolution of modernizing development has brought the costs of revolution, but it has also brought resources for new adjustments. If the governments that proudly assumed new sovereignty, and the international agencies that have tried to help them, have had to realize that they were wrestling with forces beyond their ready control, the capacities of populations to find ways of coping nevertheless have been revealed.

An awareness that we are engaged in a long, complex, and perilous course of social change should be a great stimulus to social scientific investigation. Knowing that deliberately planned and organized development programs have severe limitations gives rise to fresh perceptions of what is properly policy-relevant research, as does our awareness that the public agenda at any given time is not a sure guide to the complexities of social reality. Social scientists who wish to do some evident good in the world must maintain a certain ambivalence: They must not scorn to serve the present aims and efforts of governments and people, but must stay open to what now seems unpleasantly distracting or dispiriting. I congratulate the symposium participants on meeting this test of commitment.

References

Caldwell, J. C. "Education as a Factor in Mortality Decline: An Examination of Nigerian Data." *Population Studies,* 1979, *33* (3), 395-413.

Caldwell, J. C. "Mass Education as a Determinant of the Timing of Fertility Decline." *Population and Development Review,* 1980, *6* (2), 225-256.

Edwards, E., and Todaro, M. "Education and Employment in Developing Countries." In F. C. Ward (Ed.), *Education and Development Reconsidered/The Ballagio Conference Paper.* New York: Praeger, 1974.

Moock, J. "Pragmatism and the Primary School: The Case of a Non-Rural Village." In D. Court and P. G. Dharm (Eds.), *Education, Society and Development: New Perspectives from Kenya.* Oxford: Oxford University Press, 1974.

Pain, M. (Untitled article), *Le Monde,* November 15/16, 1981.

Francis X. Sutton is deputy vice-president of the Ford Foundation in New York. In his many years with the Ford Foundation, Dr. Sutton has traveled widely in the developing world and has been engaged in the support of numerous policy initiatives for children and education.

The editor of this sourcebook presents a brief bibliography for researchers interested in learning more about the connections between child development and international development.

Sources of Additional Information

Daniel A. Wagner

As mentioned in the Editor's Notes, there are few persons working directly at the interface between child development and international development. Therefore, interested readers will need to consult the related research literatures to gain a deeper understanding of work in this challenging area. Many of the relevant research findings are embedded in documents that treat either child development or policy issues, but usually not both. Nevertheless, a reasonable amount of information does exist both in journals and in books. There follows a selected listing of publications that treat issues directly or indirectly within the areas of child development and international development.

Journals

Child Development

Theoretical and Empirical. *Child Development, Developmental Psychology, Human Development, Developmental Review.*

Cross-Cultural/Anthropological. *Journal of Cross-Cultural Psychology, International Journal of Psychology, American Anthropologist, Ethos: Journal of Psychological Anthropology, International Journal of Behavioral Development, Revista Interamericana de Psicología, Enfance, British Journal of Developmental Psychology.*

International Development

Theoretical and Empirical. *International Development Review, Journal of Developing Areas, Institute of Development Studies Review, Journal of Development Studies, Economic Development and Cultural Change, Third World Development.*
Education. *Comparative Education Review, International Review of Education.*

Publications and Addresses

IDRC Reports (International Development Research Centre, Box 8500, Ottawa, Canada K1G 3H9)
Working papers and other reports of the World Bank (World Bank, 1818 H Street NW, Washington, D.C. 20433)
Prospects and *Notes: Comments on Child, Family and Community* (UNESCO, 7 Place de Fontenoy, 75700 Paris, France)
Occasional reports and documentation from the United Nations Children's Fund (UNICEF, 866 United Nations Plaza, New York, NY 10017)
Occasional reports from the Ford Foundation (320 E. 43rd St., New York, NY 10017)

Recent Volumes on Cross-Cultural Child Development and Related Issues

Dasen, P. (Ed.). *Piagetian Psychology: Cross-Cultural Contributions.* New York: Gardner, 1977.
Dasen, P., Inhelder, B., Lavallee, M., and Retschitski, J. *Naissance de l'intelligence chez l'enfant baoule du Côte d'Ivoire.* Berne: Hans Huber, 1978.
Field, T. M., Sostek, A. M., Vietze, P., and Leiderman, P. H. (Eds.). *Culture and Early Interactions.* Hillsdale, N.J.: Erlbaum, 1981.
Leiderman, P. H., Tulkin, S. R., and Rosenfeld, A. *Culture and Infancy.* New York: Academic Press, 1977.
Munroe, R. H., Munroe, R. L., and Whiting, B. B. (Eds.). *Handbook of Cross-Cultural Human Development.* New York: Garland, 1981.
Segall, M. H. *Cross-Cultural Psychology.* Monterey, Calif.: Brooks-Cole, 1979.
Super, C. M., and Harkness, S. (Eds.). *Anthropological Perspectives on Child Development,* New Directions for Child Development, no. 8. San Francisco: Jossey-Bass, 1980.
Triandis, H. C. (Ed.). *Handbook of Cross-Cultural Psychology,* Vols. 1-6. Boston: Allyn & Bacon, 1979-80.
UNESCO. *Childhood Inequities and Development.* Paris: UNESCO/University of Qatar, 1982.
Wagner, D. A., and Stevenson, H. W. (Eds.). *Cultural Perspectives in Child Development.* San Francisco: W. H. Freeman, 1982.
Werner, E. E. *Cross-Cultural Child Development.* Monterey, Calif.: Brooks-Cole, 1979.

Daniel A. Wagner is associate professor of human development in the Graduate School of Education, University of Pennsylvania. He is primarily interested in child development in the Third World and is currently involved in a four-year research project on the acquisition and maintenance of literacy in Morocco. With Harold W. Stevenson, he edited Cultural Perspectives on Child Development *(Freeman, 1982).*

Index

A

Abbott, J., 60, 72
Abou-Gamrah, H., 33n, 42
Acharya, M., 72
Africa: child labor in, 92-93, 104; children without families in, 16, 20-21; fertility in, 47; indigenous education in, 79; infant and child mortality in, 31, 33, 110; maternal employment in, 58; slum dwelling in, 8; urban migration in, 6, 9. *See also* individual nations
Aghajamian, A., 91-92
Aguirre, A., 62, 71, 75
Ahmed, M., 77, 83
Alfonja, S., 62, 72
American Association for the Advancement of Science, 3, 107n
Anderson, C. A., 38, 80, 83
Anker, R., 35, 36, 39, 42
Anti-Slavery Society for the Protection of Human Rights, 87, 92
Anzalone, S. J., 81, 82, 83
Argentina, urban migration in, 8, 10
Aries, P., 88, 106
Arriaga, E. E., 30n, 32n, 42
Asia: child labor in, 98; children without families in, 16, 20-21; fertility in, 47; infant and child mortality in, 30, 32; slum dwelling in, 8; urban migration in, 6, 8, 9. *See also* individual nations
Austin, J. E., 11-12, 25

B

Balderston, J. B., 66, 71, 72
Bamberger, M., 60, 74
Banarjee, S., 92
Bangladesh: child labor in, 93-94; maternal employment in, 59, 61; slum dwelling in, 8
Battad, J. P., 63, 72
Behrman, J. R., 30, 37, 40, 42, 62, 63, 72
Bekombo, M., 92-93, 104
Belize, maternal employment in, 59

Benería, L. 58, 72
Bernstein, S. 35, 37, 40, 43
Beuf, D., 89, 106
Bittencourt, S., 72
Bloch, M. N., 62, 73
Blumberg, R. L., 58, 59, 71, 72, 73
Bolivia, infant and child mortality in, 30
Boserup, E., 57, 58, 73
Botswana, Republic of, 42; infant and child mortality in, 33
Boulier, B., 29, 30, 36, 40, 42
Bourdieu, P., 78, 83
Bowman, M. J., 80, 83
Brazil: children without families in, 16, 20; slum dwelling in, 8
Breastfeeding: and infant and child mortality, 40-41; and maternal employment, 61; in urban slums, 12-13
Bromley, R., 93
Bronfenbrenner, U., 46, 54
Brown, G., 80, 83
Bruner, J. S., 78, 84
Butz, W. P., 35, 36, 37, 40, 41, 42, 61, 73, 96-97
Buvinic, M., 24, 25

C

Cabañero, T. A., 61, 62, 73
Cain, M., 61, 73, 87, 93-94, 104
Caldwell, J. C., 46, 47, 54, 109, 110, 112
California Polytechnic State University, 57n
Camara, F., 74
CARE, 1
Caribbean: children without families in, 16; women-headed households in, 24
Chamratrithirong, A., 30n, 42
Chan, P., 87, 94
Chaudhury, R. H., 59, 73
Chavez, M. L., 61, 73
Cherry, F. F., 57, 73
Child development: anthropological approach to, 45-55; cross-cultural studies of, 114; cultural models of, 51; and international development, 45-46; jour-

Child development *(continued)*
nals on, 113; structural constraints on, 1-2
Child labor: annotated bibliography on, 91-106; approaches to, 87-88; and child work, defined, 90-91; definitions in, 88-91
Child Welfare Council (Costa Rica), 19
Children: adjustments to urban migration by, 10; adversities multiple for, 11; anxieties of moving for, 13-14; defined, 88-89; exposure to mortality by, 29-33; without families, 15-21; indigenous education and literacy for, 77-85; malnutrition, poor health, and mortality of, 11-13; and maternal employment, 57-75; in slums and squatter areas, 11-15; in urban areas, 7, 9; and urban migration, 5-26; *See also* Infant and child mortality
Chile: child labor in, 95-96, 104; infant and child mortality in, 30; slum dwelling in, 8
China, urban migration in, 8, 9
Chinas, B., 74
Clanchy, M. T., 80, 83
Clapp, J., 101
Clark, C., 59, 62, 73
Cochrane, S. H., 3, 27-43, 46, 47, 48, 50, 52, 54, 60, 66, 73, 108, 109, 110
Cole, M., 80, 81, 84
Colombia: child labor in, 93; children without families in, 19; infant and child mortality in, 30, 34, 39, 41; maternal employment in, 71; slum dwelling in, 8
Coombs, P. H., 77, 83
Cornelius, W. A., 22, 23, 25
Costa Rica: children without families in, 19; infant and child mortality in, 30; revolution in, 19
Costin, L., 94-95
Council of the Child (El Salvador), 19
Cousins, W. J., 23, 25
Crèches, in urban slums, 14-15

D

Dalela, S. C., 95
Daniel, J. C., 95
Dasen, P., 114
DaVanzo, J., 30*n*, 35, 37, 40, 41, 42, 61, 73
Davies, E., 95
Davis, K., 6, 25

De la Luz Silva, M., 87, 89, 95-96, 104
De Mause, L., 88, 106
Developing countries. *See* Third World countries
Dominican Republic: children without families in, 19; infant and child mortality in, 30
Doolittle, F., 105
Dube, L., 96, 104

E

Easy, W., 96
Eaton, E. L., 57, 73
Ecuador, infant and child mortality in, 30
Education: benefits of, 109-110; blocks to, 14; indigenous, 77-85; in urban slums, 14-15; for women, 13, 23-24, 28-33, 40, 109-110; of women, and fertility, 46-54
Edwards, E., 109, 112
Egero, B., 31*n*, 42
Egypt: child labor in, 97, 102; indigenous education in, 79; infant and child mortality in, 33
Eickelman, D., 79, 83
El Salvador: children without families in, 19; infant and child mortality in, 30
Employment, maternal: and alternative caretakers, 61, 70; analysis of, 57-75; and breastfeeding, 61; changes in, 58-59; competence and confidence related to, 60; definition of, 58-59, 64-66; direct effects of, 59-61; and family economic level, 62, 71; INCAP study of, 63-71; and income increase, 59; interpretation of, 69-71; and marital status, 62; and maternal status, 59-60; and mother's characteristics, 61-62, 66-67, 68, 70; and prior conditions, 61-62; regression analysis of, 67, 69-71; research on, 58-59, 62-63; statistical analyses of, 66-67; and time for children, 60-61; at time of birth, 70-71
Engle, P. L., 3, 57-75, 81, 83, 96-97, 108
Ethiopia, infant and child mortality in, 31
Europe: fertility in, 47; slum dwelling in, 8; urban migration in, 9. *See also* individual nations
Evanson, R. E., 59, 73

F

Fagley, R. M., 58, 73
Fair Labor Standards Act of 1938, 101
Fanale, R., 74
Ferguson, C. A., 80, 83
Fertility: anthropological approach to, 45–55; and demographic transition stages, 48–50; and education of women, 46–54; historical context of, 47; and maternal attention, 51–52, 53; and mothers' schooling, 52–53; and parental investment strategies, 50–51
Field, T. M., 54, 114
Ford Foundation, 46, 77n, 114
France, child labor in, 97–98
Freire, M., 66, 72
Freire, P., 80, 83

G

Gallimore, R., 61, 75, 106
Gambia, infant and child mortality in, 31
Gay, J., 79, 83
Germain, A., 60, 73
Ghana: infant and child mortality in, 31; maternal employment in, 59, 62
Gojman de Millan, S., 74
Goody, J., 80, 83
Gopolan, M., 97
Goyder, C., 23, 25
Graff, H., 80, 83
Green, K., 81, 84
Greenfield, P., 78, 83
Greiner, T. H., 61, 63, 73
Guatemala: infant and child mortality in, 28, 30, 38; maternal employment in, 58, 60, 61, 62, 63–67, 108
Gurugé, A., 79, 83
Gwatkins, D. R., 27, 42

H

Habicht, J. P., 30, 35, 40, 42, 64, 73, 74
Haggerty, P. A., 61, 62, 71, 74
Haiti, maternal employment in, 61, 71
Hamilton, C., 97
Harkness, S., 114
Harman, D., 80, 82, 83
Harvard Graduate School of Education, 45n
Head Start, expertise for, 2
Health, poor, in urban slums, 11–13
Heath, S., 81, 83

Henin, R. A., 31n, 42
Heyneman, S., 81–82, 83
Heywood, C., 97–98
Hill, K., 32, 42
Hiskett, M., 80, 83
Ho, T., 61, 74
Hoffman, L. W., 60, 74
Hollnsteiner, M. R., 3, 5–26, 110
Honduras: children without families in, 19; infant and child mortality in, 30
Hong Kong: child labor in, 96, 99, 103; infant and child mortality in, 32; slum dwelling in, 8
Howrigan, G., 52, 55
Hull, T., 87, 89, 90, 98, 104
Hunter, S. S. J., 82, 83

I

India: child labor in, 92, 95, 96, 97, 99, 100, 103, 104, 105–106; crèches in, 15; fertility in, 47; infant and child mortality in, 13, 35, 37; maternal employment in, 59, 63; urban migration in, 8, 23
Indigenous education: analysis of, 77–85; as cultural capital, 78–79; defined, 78; implications of, 82–83; in Islamic schools, 78–80; literacy instruction in, 80–82
Indonesia: indigenous education in, 79; infant and child mortality in, 32; slum dwelling in, 8
Industrial Revolution, and child labor, 88, 97–98, 101
Infant and child mortality: analysis of, 27–43; and breastfeeding, 40–41; determinants of, studies on, 35–41; and education of parents, 28–33, 40; implications for, 41; and medical facilities, 40; multivariate analysis of, 29–33; and proportion of children surviving, 33–35, 38–39; and sex of child, 35; socioeconomic differentials in, 28–33; in urban slums, 11–13
Inhelder, B., 114
Institute for Family Welfare (Colombia), 19
Institute of Nutrition in Central America and Panama (INCAP), 63–71
International Center for Research on Women (ICRW), 57, 74
International development: and child development, 45–46; journals on, 114

International Development Research Centre (IDRC), 8*n,* 77*n,* 82, 84, 114
International Labor Office (ILO), 93, 98, 100
International Textile, Garment, and Leather Workers Federation, 98-99
International Year of the Child, 46
Iran, child labor in, 91-92
Islamic schools: indigenous education in, 78-80; literacy instruction in, 80-82
Iyer, K. V., 99

J

Java, child labor in, 102
Jelliffe, E. F. P., 74
Jordan, infant and child mortality in, 30
Journals, 113-114
Jurmo, P., 80, 84

K

Kenya, Republic of, 42; fertility in, 51-52; infant and child mortality in, 28, 31, 33, 36, 39; urbanization in, 8, 110
Khanam, S., 61, 73
Khorshed, A. B. M., 94
Kitteringham, J., 99
Klein, R. E., 60, 64, 73, 74
Knight, W. J., 99
Knodel, J., 30*n,* 42, 47, 52, 54, 55
Knowles, J. C., 34, 35, 36, 38, 39, 42
Korea, Republic of: indigenous education in, 79; infant and child mortality in, 32, 36, 40; urban migration in, 8, 10
Kuchero, T., 100
Kulandaiswamy, V., 97
Kumar, S. K., 59, 74
Kurz, D., 89, 106

L

Landes, W., 100
Laquian, A. A., 8, 25
Latin America: children without families in, 15-21; fertility in, 47; hopeful signs in, 19-20; infant and child mortality in, 30; maternal employment in, 62; prevention programs in, 18-19; slum dwelling in, 8; urban migration in, 6, 8, 9, 17-18. *See also* individual nations

Lavallee, M., 114
Lave, J., 78, 83
Lee, D. L. P., 61, 73
Leiderman, P. H., 54, 114
Lenkerd, B., 74
Lerner, D., 80, 84
Leslie, J., 29, 35, 42
Levin, R., 57*n*
LeVine, R. A., 3, 45-55, 60, 70, 74, 109
Levinson, F. S., 63, 74
Liberia, indigenous education in, 79
Literacy: defined, 80, 81; imperative for, 111; implications for, 82-83; indigenous education for, 77-85; in modern and indigenous schools, 80-82
Lopez, M. E., 14, 25
Lotfi, A., 77*n,* 78, 79, 80, 84
Loucky, J., 61, 73

M

Maccan, S. Z., 60, 74
McGuire, J., 60, 74
Mahadevan, M., 15, 25
Majayata, A. R. A., 30*n,* 43
Malaysia: child labor in, 94; infant and child mortality in, 30, 36, 37, 41; maternal employment in, 61
Malaysia Family Life Survey, 41
Malnutrition, in urban slums, 11-13
Marla, S., 100
Marshall, S. M. L., 59, 75
Maternal employment. *See* Employment, maternal
Mehra, K., 3, 27-43, 52, 60, 108, 110
Mejía Piveral, V., 64, 74
Mendelievich, E., 100-101
Messick, B. M., 79, 84
Mexico: children without families in, 16, 19; fertility in, 47; urban migration in, 8, 22-23
Migration. *See* Urban migration
Minge-Kalman, W., 101
Ministry of Social Welfare (Brazil), 20
Ministry of Social Welfare (Nicaragua), 20
Mitchell, D., 101
Moock, J., 110, 112
Moore, E. B., 3, 84, 87-106
Morice, A., 87, 90, 101, 104
Morocco: child labor in, 92; indigenous education in, 79-80, 81; slum dwelling in, 8

Mortality. *See* Infant and child mortality
Mueller, E., 87, 89, 102
Munroe, R. H., 114
Munroe, R. L., 114
Murphy, D., 5, 25

N

Nag, M., 48, 55, 102
Nagi, M., 87, 102
Nahar, S., 61, 73
National Board of Family Welfare (Honduras), 19
National Child Welfare Foundation (Brazil), 20
National Council of the Child (Dominican Republic), 19
National Institute of Education (NIE), 1*n*, 77*n*
National Institutes of Health, 1*n*
National Program of Integrated Family Services (Mexico), 19
National Science Foundation, 45*n*
Nepal: child labor in, 102; infant and child mortality in, 30, 35, 37, 38, 40
Nerlove, S. B., 64, 74
New, R., 52, 55
Nicaragua: children without families in, 20; infant and child mortality in, 30, 37; maternal employment in, 63; revolution in, 19
NICHD, 77*n*
Nieves, I., 72, 74
Nigeria: child labor in, 104-105; infant and child mortality in, 33, 110; maternal employment in, 62
Noesjirwan, J., 80, 84

O

O'Halloran, G., 80, 84
O'Hara, D. J., 29, 35, 40, 42, 43
Organizations: collaboration with specialists by, 3; international, 1
Osterman, P., 91, 102-103
Oxenham, J., 80, 84

P

Pacific Islands, urban migration in, 9
Pain, M., 111. 112
Pakistan: infant and child mortality in, 32, 38; slum dwelling in, 8

Paqueo, V. B., 29, 30, 36, 40, 42
Paraguay, infant and child mortality in, 30
Paton, A., 5, 25
Peet, R. C., 102
Peru: child labor in, 105; infant and child mortality in, 30; slum dwelling in, 8
Philippines: infant and child mortality in, 32; maternal employment in, 60, 61, 62, 63; urban migration in, 8, 13, 23
Plumb, J. H., 88, 106
Policy: changes in relevance of, 108-109; relevance of, 107-112; research interface with, 22-24
Popkin, B. M., 60, 63, 74
Population Council Project on Women's Schooling and Fertility, 45*n*
Porter, R., 87, 103
Prateep, K., 14
Premi, M., 103
Preston, S. H., 29, 34, 35, 43
Project on Human Potential, 45*n*
Prosser, R. C., 77, 83

Q

Quranic schools. *See* Islamic schools

R

Ramachandaran, K. V., 31*n*, 43
Reder, S., 81, 84
Reining, P., 60, 74
Repetto, R. G., 87, 103
Republic of... *See* entries under distinguishing national name, such as Botswana, Republic of
Research, policy relevance of, 107-112
Research-policy interface, for urban migration, 22-24
Retschitski, J., 114
Rhodesia, Republic of, 33*n*, 43
Riccuiti, H. N., 62, 74
Richman, A., 52, 55
Ridker, R. C., 89, 106
Rivera, C. M., 60, 62, 74
Roberts, J. M., 64, 74
Rodgers, G., 87, 89, 90, 104
Rosenfeld, A., 114
Rosenzweig, J. R., 34, 39, 41, 43
Rosenzweig, M. R., 87, 104
Roskies, D., 79, 84
Ross, G., 78, 84

S

Safilios-Rothschild, C., 59, 74
Sandell, G., 13, 25
Sandell, M., 13, 25
Save the Children, 1
Schildkrout, E., 89, 91, 104–105
Schultz, T. P., 34, 39, 41, 43
Scribner, S., 80, 81, 84
Scrimshaw, S., 48, 54, 55
Seeley, K. M., 84
Segall, M. H., 114
Sembajwe, I. S. L., 33n, 43
Sen, G., 58, 72
Sénégal, République du, 43; indigenous education in, 79–80; infant and child mortality in, 31; maternal employment in, 62
Sengupta, P., 105
Sharman, A., 71, 74
Shinohara, I., 74
Sierra Leone, infant and child mortality in, 31
Silvey, J., 77, 84
Simmons, G., 35, 37, 40, 43
Simmons, J., 77, 80, 84
Simonen, M., 66, 72
Slums and squatter areas: children in, 11–15; extent of, 8; paradoxical attraction of, 21–22
Smith, S., 105
Social Science Research Council, 77n
Solmon, L. C., 100
Solon, F. S., 63, 74
Sostek, A. M., 54, 114
Spencer Foundation, 1n, 45n, 77n
Spolsky, B., 81, 84
Spratt, J., 84
Sri Lanka, infant and child mortality in, 36, 40
Standing, G., 87, 89, 90, 104
Stavrakis, O., 59, 75
Stern, D., 105
Stevenson, H. W., 1n, 114
Sudan, infant and child mortality in, 31
Super, C. M., 114
Survival, improvements in, 1. *See also* Infant and child mortality
Sutton, F. X., 3, 107–112

T

Taçon, P., 3, 5–26, 110
Tambiah, S. J., 79, 84

Tanzania, infant and child mortality in, 31
Tawiah, E. O., 31n, 43
Taylor, C., 63, 75
Thailand: indigenous education in, 79; infant and child mortality in, 30; urban migration in, 8, 14, 23
Third World countries: child development specialists needed in, 3; child labor in, 87–106; expertise in, 2; fertility and child development in, 45–55; indigenous education and literacy in, 77–85; infant and child mortality in, 27–43; maternal employment and children's welfare in, 57–75; policy relevance for, 107–112; urban migration in, 5–26
Tienda, M., 87, 89–90, 105
Tinker, I., 74
Todaro, M., 109, 112
Townsend, J., 60, 73
Triandis, H. C., 114
Tripp, R. B., 59, 62, 75
Trussell, T. J., 29, 34, 35, 43
Tulkin, S. R., 114
Turkey, slum dwelling in, 8

U

Uganda, Republic of, 43; infant and child mortality in, 31
UNESCO, 1, 3, 4, 81, 84, 114
Ungsongtham, P., 14, 25
United Kingdom, child labor in, 95, 96, 99
United Nations, 6, 10, 25
United Nations Housing Survey, 8n
United Nations International Children's Emergency Fund (UNICEF), 1, 9n, 13, 20, 25, 114
United Nations Population Division, 7n
United States: child labor in, 94–95, 100, 101, 102–103, 105; illiteracy in, 82; maternal employment in, 57, 60
Urban migration: analysis of, 5–26; and people-oriented policies, 22–24; reasons for, 10, 17, 21–22; research-policy interface for, 22–24; research priorities for, 24; trends in, 6–11

V

Van de Walle, E., 47, 55
van Leer Foundation, Bernard, 45n

Venezuela: maternal employment in, 60; slum dwelling in, 8
Vietze, P., 54, 114
Vlassoff, M., 87, 105-106
Von Elm, B., 24, 25
Vygotsky, L., 78, 84

W

Wagner, D. A., 1-4, 54, 57*n*, 77-85, 108, 111, 113-115
Weber, M., 107
Weisner, T. S., 61, 75, 106
Werner, E. E., 114
White, B., 102
Whiting, B. B., 114
Wilson, A. B., 66, 71, 72, 75
Wilson, E. O., 51, 55
Wolfe, B. L., 30, 37, 40, 42, 62, 63, 72
Women: education for, 13, 23-24, 28-33, 40, 46-54, 109-110; employment of, 57-75; and urban migration, 10, 12-13, 15, 18, 23-24
Wood, D., 78, 84

Work, defined, 89-90, 96. *See also* Child labor; Employment, maternal
World Bank, 11, 114
World Health Organization (WHO), 1, 27
Wray, J. D., 62, 71, 75

Y

Yarbrough, C., 60, 73
Yarbrough, D. S., 64, 74
Yemen Arab Republic, indigenous education in, 79
Yoo, H. J., 79, 84
Youssef, N. H., 24, 25

Z

Zaire: indigenous education in, 111; slum dwelling in, 8
Zambia, infant and child mortality in, 31
Zamir, I., 106
Zimbabwe, infant and child mortality in, 33